CONTEMPORARY
QUILTS

CONTEMPORARY QUILTS

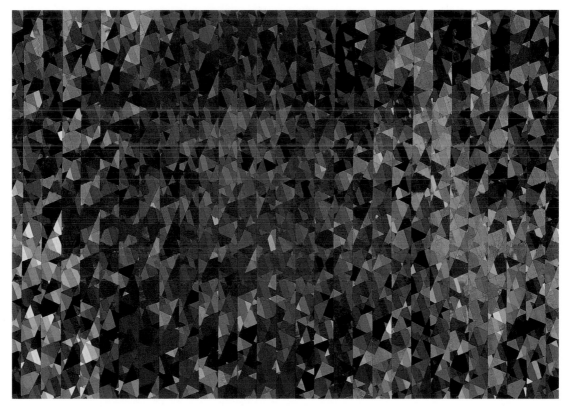

JOY SAVILLE

Quilt National, 1997

Coproduced By Lark Books & The Dairy Barn Cultural Arts Center

Lark Books

Asheville, North Carolina

Project Director: Hilary Morrow Fletcher
Photographer: Brian Blauser
Art Director and production: Kathleen Holmes
Editor: Dawn Cusick

Additional photography provided by Karen Bell (page 47),
David Caras (pages 14 and 69), Pam Monfort (pages 79, 82,
and 83), Sharon Risedorf (pages 10, 26, and 89), Roger Sands (page 42),
and William Taylor (page 84) .

Library of Congress Cataloging-in-Publication Data

Quilt National (1997 : Athens, Ohio)
    Contemporary Quilts : Quilt National, 1997 / Quilt National
        p.   cm.
    "Coproduced by Lark Books & the Dairy Barn Cultural Arts Center."
    Includes index.
    ISBN 1-887374-35-3
    1. Quilts—United States—History—20th century—Exhibitions.
2. Quilts—History—20th century—Exhibitions. I. Dairy Barn
Southeastern Ohio Cultural Arts Center. II. Title.
NK9112.Q5 1997
746.46'0973'07477197—dc21   97-7736
                        CIP

10 9 8 7 6 5 4 3 2 1

First Edition

Published by Lark Books
50 College St.
Asheville, NC 28801, USA

Distributed by Random House, Inc., in the United States, Canada, the
    United Kingdom, Europe,and Asia
Distributed in Australia by Capricorn Link (Australia) Pty Ltd.,
    P.O. Box 6651, Baulkham Hills Business Centre, NSW 2153, Australia
Distributed in New Zealand by Tandem Press Ltd., 2 Rugby Rd.,
    Birkenhead, Auckland, New Zealand

Printed in Hong Kong

ISBN 1-887374-35-3

*From top to bottom, details of
quilts by Bonnie Peterson-Tucker,
Niki Bonnett, Kyoung Ae Cho,
Susan Shie & James Acord, and
Bernie Rowell.*

CONTENTS

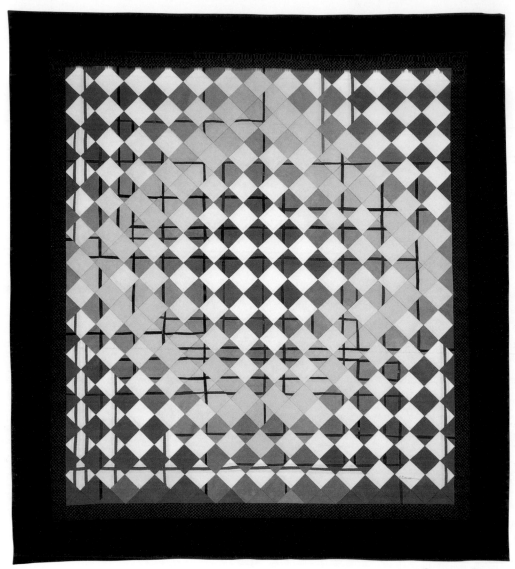

CATHERINE DAWSON

FOREWORD

For the tenth time in nearly 20 years the Dairy Barn Southeastern Ohio Cultural Arts Center has had the honor and the privilege of presenting a **Quilt National** exhibition. We believe that the works in this collection are among the finest, most exciting quilts being made anywhere in the world.

It might be said that the story of **Quilt National '97** is in the numbers. More works were submitted for this **Quilt National** than ever before. The entrants represented more countries than ever before. The selected works represent more first-time exhibitors than ever before. And it is likely that portions of this **Quilt National** will be seen at more touring venues and by more people than ever before. The 83 quilts in **Quilt National '97** provide conclusive evidence that the art form is alive and well.

In making this statement, I recognize the critical roles that have been played by many individuals. These are the people whose efforts and contributions may not be immediately obvious as one steps into the gallery or opens this book. However, it would be impossible to over-exaggerate their importance, for without them, there would surely be no **Quilt National**.

To say that jurors Nancy Halpern, Jason Pollen, and Joan Schulze undertook a difficult job would be a gross understatement. Their collective experience and vision has yielded an exhibition of incomparable strength and diversity.

As you might expect, the financial resources necessary to produce a **Quilt National** exhibition are significant. The Dairy Barn has been blessed with the friendship and support of several corporations, organizations and individuals: Ms. Donna Wilder and the Fairfield Processing Corporation, maker of Poly-fil fiber products; Mr. Tadanobu Seto and *Quilts Japan* magazine; Ms. Robin Steele and Cranston Print Works Company, maker of VIP fabrics; Ms. Camille Cook and Friends of Fiber Art International; Ms. Penny McMorris and the Electric Quilt Company; Ms. Cathy Rasmussen and Studio Art Quilt Associates; Dr. Wayne Lawson and the Ohio Arts Council; Mayor Ric Abel and the City of Athens; and dozens of generous artists and private individuals.

Our gratitude also goes to publisher Rob Pulleyn and the staff of Altamont Press for their incredible skill as well as their gentle guidance and patient support during the preparation of this book. They make the process seem almost easy.

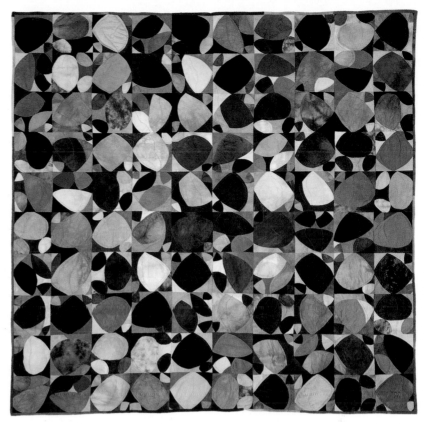

CONNIE SCHEELE

We are very fortunate, too, to have the support of countless members of the Athens community. Without our corps of dedicated and talented volunteers, each member of the Dairy Barn staff would need at least 50 pairs of arms and legs, and the ability to be in 20 places at the same time.

The Dairy Barn Cultural Arts Center is committed to presenting the best arts, crafts, and cultural heritage of our region. This has been accomplished through a variety of exhibits, educational programs and festivals, the Touring Exhibits Program, and, most recently, by establishing a site on the World Wide Web (http://www.eurekanet.com/~dbarn). Visitors to our cyberspace site can learn about all of our programs, including **Beadworks**, our newest juried biennial international exhibition that will make its debut in summer, 1998.

Quilt National continues to be a joy for all of us associated with the Dairy Barn. We hope that those who read this book and visit the exhibition will sense our pleasure and will share in it as they experience the wonders and excitement of **Quilt National '97**.

Susan Cole Urano
Executive Director
Dairy Barn Southeastern Ohio Cultural Arts Center

SUSAN WEBB LEE

INTRODUCTION

Many questions run through my mind as I think about what might be an appropriate introduction to the catalog of this, the tenth biennial **Quilt National** exhibition. Can it really be almost two decades since **Quilt National** began? Have I really been the project director for the past eight **Quilt Nationals**? How do I feel about the evolution of "the quilt as art" that I have witnessed? The answers are *Yes, Yes*, and, *It has been an honor and a privilege to observe and (hopefully) to foster the growth of something that is obviously important to a great many people.*

Foremost among the joys associated with this job has been the pleasure of seeing the more than 9,000 entries submitted since 1980 when my involvement with **Quilt National** began. I never cease to be amazed by the variety of the entrants' unique visions. I marvel, too, at how each panel of **Quilt National** jurors has managed to assemble a broad, yet remarkably cohesive, collection of works. Those who see **Quilt National '97** will have the opportunity to see how today's quilt makers are building on the foundations created by generations of talented and skilled artists. One need only compare the works chosen for the first **Quilt National**, in 1979, with those in this volume to know that the art form has been irrevocably altered.

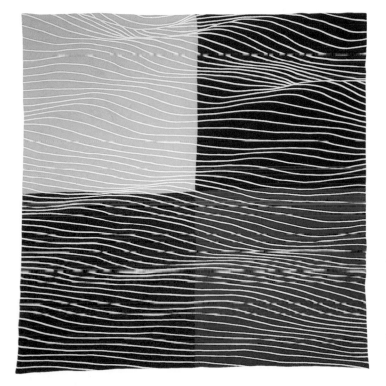

ANNELIESE JAROS

Today's quilts may be made entirely by hand or by a combination of hand and machine techniques. They may incorporate commercial fabrics or specially created materials. They may make us smile with thoughts of carefree childhood or stir darker feelings as we ponder the consequences of terminal illness. Today's quilt makers are simply doing what has always been done: making choices and, thereby, shaping available materials into objects that give us a glimpse of something that is meaningful to the quilt maker. While works of painted vinyl or photocopied fabrics may bear little apparent resemblance to what people envision at the mention of the word "quilt," they are, in fact, products of the very same creative energy responsible for great-grandmother's Flower Garden or Double Wedding Ring. (Just imagine what grandmother might have done with a laser printer or color copier!) Quilts have always been personal and artistic expressions, and the works in this collection are no exception.

Another joy associated with this job is the opportunity to talk to many of the tens of thousands of visitors who travel (often great distances) to see a **Quilt National** exhibition at the Dairy Barn. Here again, a question comes to mind: Why do we expect a quilt made at the dawn of the 21st century to be like one made fifty or a hundred years earlier? We certainly don't expect a brand new car to look like a Model T. Computers, color photocopiers, AIDS, and the Greenhouse effect were unknown as recently as a generation ago, and all have had a profound impact on today's quilts.

The more I learn about quilts, the more I become convinced that a great many new and old quilts are artistic expressions. They, like paintings and sculptures, represent the interaction of four basic elements: the available materials and techniques, the individual (quilt) maker's creativity, the nature of the (quilt) maker's world, and the (quilt) maker's visions of and experiences with that world.

Increasing numbers of quilt makers and art lovers are becoming aware that innovative art quilts now flourish and coexist with the functional bed covers that have long enjoyed popularity. Although some might credit me and the Dairy Barn Cultural Arts Center for this situation, we are but "an insignificant little wheel" that would spin aimlessly in the absence of so many others whose efforts and contributions make everything possible: the sponsors who provide much needed financial support, the jurors who make unimaginably difficult choices, the volunteers who enable the exhibition to happen, the visitors who provide the reason for **Quilt National**, and, most importantly, the artists who so generously share their work with us.

Our goal is to produce an exhibition that accurately represents the diversity, quality, and creativity of artists who have chosen to express themselves in this medium of layered, stuffed, and stitched fabric. We hope that after studying the images in this collection you will gain a new appreciation for and an understanding of the nature of the art quilt as we approach the new millennium.

Hilary Morrow Fletcher
Project Director

JURORS' STATEMENTS

JOAN SCHULZE

So much has been written about the jury system. To consent to this collaborative effort one has to be imbued with a great deal of faith. It is difficult territory, and in some ways relates to making quilts. We the jurors are given many choices (pieces) to make up a show (sew the pieces together to make a larger whole) which will reveal the diversity of work being done today. Each piece must stand on its own, but we also hope they work together to create a sense of excitement. We wanted the quilts to be good and sincere expressions, and we worked to find the inventive and the original from nearly 600 makers submitting 1254 quilts.

Each artist used the camera to capture what he/she knew to be there. The range of success at this task was enormous. We cannot see what the film did not record. Some of the flaws noted in this jurying included focus problems, dim lighting, busy backgrounds, and irrelevant or distracting details. Even the best slides can only hint at what the real object must be. And so, using an admittedly imperfect system, we looked at the submitted works over and over again over a period of days. What is the alternative? If wishes were horses, we would look at each quilt in person. This appealing idea has no hope of being realized in this situation. So we cast the show using stand-ins. This is the hard task of the juror.

What do we as jurors bring to the task? We bring our instincts, experience with the medium, and the ability to make judgements on quality of idea, color, design, and originality. Each juror comes with different hopes at what he/she will find. I personally wanted to find quilts that showed the courage to break new ground, that took an old idea and made it fresh, that moved away from the trite, the current fashion, and most of all exhibited a tone or quality that added something to this

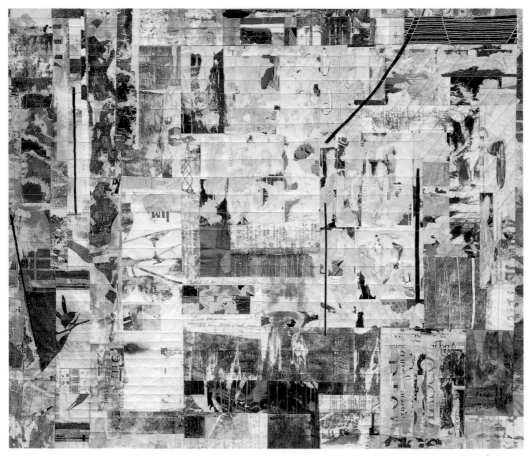

JOAN SCHULZE

PALIMPSEST

MIXED MEDIA FIBER CONSTRUCTION; 59 x 50 INCHES.

Palimpsest *is an investigation into surfaces. Images fragment; colors are revealed underneath peeling paint or paper on cloth; erasures of original drawings float between other layers reminiscent of old illuminated manuscripts. The incongruities are there to puzzle out, to make your own stories, to enjoy the complexity.*

slow, onward line of change which we call quilt history. Now the preponderance is with the hand-dyed and painted fabrics, surfaces altered using objects, transfer methods, images, and other personal marks. If one does not create these fabrics, they now can be purchased. The question still remains and has always been: to what end do we use all these tools and materials?

In an era of more is more, several quilts stand out for their daring use of simple means. Alison Whittemore's *Metaphor for a Bed*, Judy Turner's *Desert Sky* and Michael James' *Ikon* take an element and repeat it with quiet elegance. When looking at the show as a whole, these provide counterpoint to the very complex works. Artists who have taken the American staple of quilt block format and given it a rich and satisfying interpretation are exemplified by Rachel Brumer's *Bread: Staple, Fourth Removed*, Gerry Chase's *Repeat Block IV: Vessels*, Denise Linet's *Zen Circles*, and Carol Tombers' *The Southern Moon*. We may expect and want the presence of beauty. Then, when you add fun and humor on top of that you get quilts like Jane Burch Cochran's *Looking for God*, Yvonne Forman's *Einstein and Tomatoes*, and the delightful *I'm Buggin'* by Emily Parson.

There were quilts that got away. Having to keep the total to 80, hard choices were made. I will miss many of them in the show but am hopeful the makers will try again. The quilt-as-slide made the journey, and was seen and appreciated many times during the jury process. We thank you all for the opportunity to see what you are doing and wish you well.

After graduating from the University of Illinois, Joan Schulze taught school for five years and then raised a family of four children. She began making quilts more than thirty years ago, drawing on her embroidery, dyeing, and other textile techniques. Her quilts have toured in Europe, Japan, Canada, Australia, and the United States, and been shown in several major exhibitions. Joan resides in Sunnyvale, California.

JASON POLLEN

As the only non-quilter among the jurors, I approached the task with an equal amount of freedom that comes with under familiarity with the field as well as trepidation for the same reason. But art is not medium-specific, and our job was to recognize it when it presented itself. We had the daunting task of selecting 80 out of 1254 slides. This requires a great deal of trust that those slides faithfully represent the actual work. We will only know for sure that we made the "right" choices on May 23rd, when we arrive for the opening at the Dairy Barn. We viewed a surprising number of images of the Virgin of Guadalupe, the Venus of Willendorf, body parts, prints of hands, zebras, crows, fish, and text.

What strikes me deeply is the overwhelming number of quilts which embody a strong point of view, both visually and conceptually. Sometimes humorous, sometimes profoundly introspective, sometimes somewhere in between, the majority speak, sing, shout, and whisper with individual voices, almost all worthy of listening to and looking at. I feel honored to have witnessed this wealth of work, the dedication, the care, and the courage to bravely pursue a particular untrodden path.

Perhaps my only criticism concerns the tendency to put everything plus the kitchen sink into each work, and, in addition, the use of a multitude of processes as well as a myriad of colors. This overabundance of a good thing can often diminish the impact of a quilt rather than enhance it. What the three of us felt (quite often) was that a detail shot was more impressive than a full view. This might indicate that simplicity can sometimes be more effective than complexity. Many of the most arresting works are composed of relatively few, sensitively considered colors, allowing space and spaciousness to set off intriguing visual events.

Not wishing to toot my surface design horn too loudly, I cannot help notice that a significant percentage of quilters are dyeing, printing, painting, transferring, and embellishing their own fabrics. This happy symbiosis continues to be fostered by Nancy Crow and Linda Fowler's annual Quilt Surface Design Symposium, as well as the Surface Design Association, and is having a profound impact on the field. The freedom to create one's only vocabulary on cloth is leading to a more intimate connection with all the layers which compose the quilt. I anticipate that the quilt-as-art form will continue to evolve and attract the attention of a more vast and discerning audience. The quilter's needle is sharp and shiny, and like Joan of Arc's sword, poised to lead the way out of the world of the boring and the banal and onto greater glories!

Jason Pollen teaches in the fiber department at the Kansas City Art Institute and serves as president of the Surface Design Association. He has been a textile designer for Jack Lenor Larsen, Perry Ellis, Oscar de la Renta, Yves St. Laurent, Jantzen Swimwear, and Nieman-Marcus, and his designs have won numerous international awards. He resides in Kansas City, Missouri.

Detail

M EDITATION

FUSED SILK; PRINTED AND PAINTED; 480 x 12 INCHES.

The simple act of skimming smooth stones off the crests of ocean waves or of building sand castles from moist clay and silvery shells. And the repetition of those waves, the thunder in their voice, the even greater silence of the blue or gray sky. These images form the roots of all subsequent creative activities. Now, luminous silk and liquid colors and that same silence provide clues to the riddle's answer.

Installation

NANCY HALPERN

Eighteen carousels of slides — an eighteen-wheeler rumbling across the optic nerve — the necessity to reduce and compress its cargo to eighty quilts — one carousel — reeling merry-go-round — tilted-at windmill — precarious unicycle. This was the task that confronted us. How much of this year's show was pure choice, and how much determined by the process, the constraints of space in the Dairy Barn, the time to do justice to 1254 quilts, and the perils of photography? We were a compatible jury with individual agendas. Mine was to try to find a hint of "the behind" in each quilt, the depth under the surface, the meaning, history, and richness of soul hidden within its layers, the quilt that can be truly known, in fact, only to its creator. In the mad rush and tumble of images, calm quilts had great power. They held our attention. How many of these monochromatic or bicolored quilts indicated the sure and restrained hand of their makers creating subtle fields for vision and thought? How many were simply oases for tired eyes?

We were wary to avoid popular stylistic and thematic trends. (Of interest: it appeared that the Inner Children of yesteryear have metamorphosed into the Venus of Willendorf.) Icon-like central figures bearing quasi-religious messages were numerous, but we desanctified all but the most vital. Quilts of hope and renewal, commemoration or witnessing were poignant, harrowing, sobering, and inspiring, but their messages had to be conveyed through artistic and not just didactic merit. We guarded against slap-happy surface design and runaway rotary cutting. We were death on imitators.

Fresher themes indicated a resurgence of interest in nature, both in elemental subjects — water and ice, fire and ash, wind, dirt, dust — and in its intimate particulars

JASON POLLEN

— leaves, sticks, pebbles, fish. (A number of chickens fell by the wayside.) There was a running (and often humorous) commentary on domesticity — babies, baking, clothing, tea. A handful of quilts presented more urban imagery — cars, graffiti, tickets, speed.

Did we as jurors latch onto these fleeting images out of our own sympathetic reactions? Undoubtedly. Will all "the behind" I hoped to sense materialize in the reality of the quilts without the intervention or mediation of photography? What about scale? Whatever we imagined, will the actual size of each quilt diminish or enhance its projected image? Will each quilt spring into a three-dimensional entity that surpasses its two-dimensional representation?

For years my friends and I have tossed around the idea of a *Salon des Refuseés*, a parallel show to be chosen from **Quilt National's** casualties. Late Saturday night, as we drove past the charming, boarded-up railway station in downtown Athens, I heard myself suggest to the amazingly resilient and forebearing Hilary and Marvin Fletcher that this would be just the place. I would, I declared, have no trouble filling it wall-to-wall with exceptionally worthy pieces that could not be squeezed into the Dairy Barn. They had the grace to laugh.

NANCY HALPERN

FITZGERALD RAG

COTTONS AND BLENDS; MACHINE PIECED AND HAND QUILTED; 62 X 69 INCHES.

The Fitzgerald Marine Reserve, near Half Moon Bay, California, is a maze of tide-pools full of starfish, sea anemones, and sea urchins. It is sheer pleasure to slosh through the pools at low tide, finding new treasures at every step.

I'm sure Joan and Jason could act as curators for similar shows. Hilary, after all was over and done, allowed herself many sighs over personal favorites. So this **Quilt National** stands, once again, as three people's idiosyncratic gatherings from the best slides of the best work entered, a one-wheeled barrow overflowing with strong, lively, thoughtful, and colorful offerings culled with pain and regret from a huge and flourishing array of contemporary quilts.

Nancy Halpern has a BA from the University of California, Berkeley, and has studied at Radcliffe and the Boston Architectural Center. She has taught quiltmaking for more than 20 years throughout the world, including Warsaw, Poland and Kyoto, Japan. Her prizewinning contemporary quilts have been exhibited nationally and internationally in both solo and group shows and published in numerous books and magazines. She resides in Natick, Massachusetts.

Plantation, Florida

FRAN **S**KILES

BEST OF SHOW

RED LANDSCAPE

COTTON DUCK FABRIC AND WOVEN PRINTED HEMP TREATED WITH OIL STICK, ACRYLIC, AND FABRIC PAINT; MACHINE STITCHED; 63 x 52 INCHES.

My assemblages are about old, decaying materials — old wooden piers, buildings and the stuff found therein. Traditionally, I turn to landscapes for design. My thoughts and elements are abstract. The imagery I use in my quilts is from my own photography. I want the image to lose its identity and become a part of the whole.

FAIRFIELD TENTH COMMEMORATIVE PRIZE

HEAVEN'S GATE

COTTON FABRIC; MACHINE PIECED, HAND APPLIQUÉD, HAND EMBROIDERED,
HAND BEADED, AND HAND QUILTED; 82 X 82 INCHES.

I was inspired to make Heaven's Gate after viewing a television program about people's near-death experiences. I was amazed by how similar the stories were. All described themselves floating down a corridor with colorful squares of light and the glowing outline of a figure reaching out to them. All of the people reported that the experience was very peaceful and that they no longer feared death. After the show, I also felt more peaceful about death and what happens after . . . it truly is only "another horizon."

B O R G H E S E

HAND-DYED COTTON EMBELLISHED WITH PAINT AND INK; MACHINE PIECED AND
APPLIQUÉD, HAND QUILTED; 43 x 55 INCHES.

■

Borghese is meant to look like an old stucco wall: peeling, crumbling and spotted with mud.
Drawings of architectural fragments and written quotations are partially obscured by layers of paint.
The quilting outlines a street map of Rome. I want the quilt to show the layers of meaning which accu-
mulate around buildings, places, and ideas with the passage of time.

ZEN CIRCLES

COMMERCIAL AND HAND-DYED COTTON AND LINEN FABRICS; MACHINE PIECED
AND HAND QUILTED, EMBELLISHED WITH BEADS AND FOUND OBJECTS; 41 x 55
INCHES.

This quilt was inspired by Sue Bender's book Everyday Sacred. Each morning I would go into my studio to compose a "circle," and I'd wait to see how my muse would fill the void. I eagerly looked forward to the new inspiration that quickly filled the empty space on my design wall. The challenge was to take each individual "circle" and create a coherent whole.

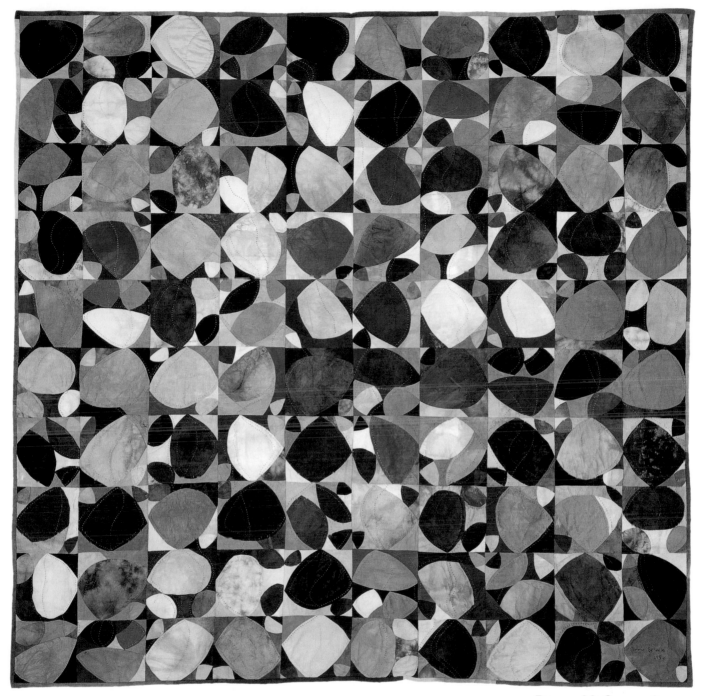

DOMINI McCARTHY AWARD

611 RIVER ROCKS

HAND-DYED COTTON FABRICS, COTTON BATTING, SILK AND COTTON QUILTING
THREADS; MACHINE PIECED AND HAND QUILTED; 60 x 60 INCHES.

*This is the third quilt in a series inspired by river rocks. I have canoed the Brule River in Northern
Wisconsin since I was a young girl, and love the look of the river rocks through clear water. After dyeing
a wide range of neutral fabrics, I felt compelled to create quilts that incorporate the wonderful colors of
nature and the fascinating shapes of the river rocks.*

A M E R I C A N I N A S I A :
A F A B R I C D I A R Y O F H O N G K O N G , T H A I L A N D ,
T H E E A S T E R N & O R I E N T A L E X P R E S S ,
S I N G A P O R E , T O K Y O , & K Y O T O

V A R I O U S F A B R I C S A N D F O U N D O B J E C T S ; P I E C E D , A P P L I Q U É D , C O L L A G E D , A N D
Q U I L T E D ; 83 X 53 I N C H E S .

In 1995, I spent four weeks in Asia. Before going, I made a diary — an American flag — from a painter's drop cloth and divided it into one "page" for each day. I expected that each day my parochial American outlook would be overlaid with uniquely Asian impressions, and I wanted to record them. The fabric diary does show some of my experiences, but, primarily, it reminds me of how this trip has changed the way I see everything. I think of as a sampler. If I could think of a technique, I tried it; if I could get a medium to stick, I used it.

S PRING

C OTTONS AND BLENDS; MACHINE PIECED AND MACHINE QUILTED;
36 X 36 INCHES.

My quilts are autobiographical and a tribute to the resilience of the human spirit. I like arranging scraps — found materials of someone else's design — into a new form. With printed, eccentric fabric I peruse chance encounters of lines and colors, and out of this dialogue with the material comes the finished product. Quilts have a history and a language of their own. I am joining the many women who have written their diaries in cloth.

W E E D S

COTTONS AND VARIOUS THREADS; MACHINE APPLIQUÉD AND MACHINE QUILTED;
42 x 42 INCHES. FROM A PRIVATE COLLECTION.

Restless weeds, persistent in their divine right to flourish. Are they calamitous pests or triumphant flowers? I'm sure they are unaware of their sinister reputation as they weave their way to the sun. Are they not as majestic as a delicately cultivated blossom? Shouldn't they be admired for their tenacious energy, determination, and shameless pride? Love them or hate them, you must be fascinated by their stunning life force and uninhibited creativity.

ELSWORTH

DYED, DISCHARGED, AND SCREEN-PRINTED FABRIC; APPLIQUÉD (DIRECT AND
REVERSE) AND EMBROIDERED, HAND QUILTED AND TIED; 70 x 70 INCHES.

The inspiration for my work is the landscape and man's mark on it. I am very aware of earlier cultures and times and how man has left behind evidence of his presence. Disclose, lay open, reveal, discover, and uncover are key words and have influenced my textile techniques. I stitch and manipulate cloth, which I use for its tactile quality, its substance, and its intimacy.

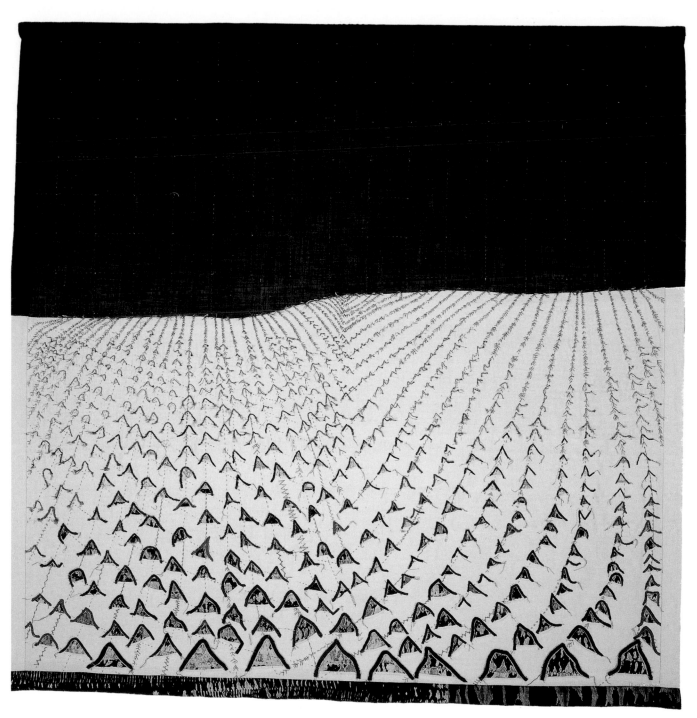

Reverse View

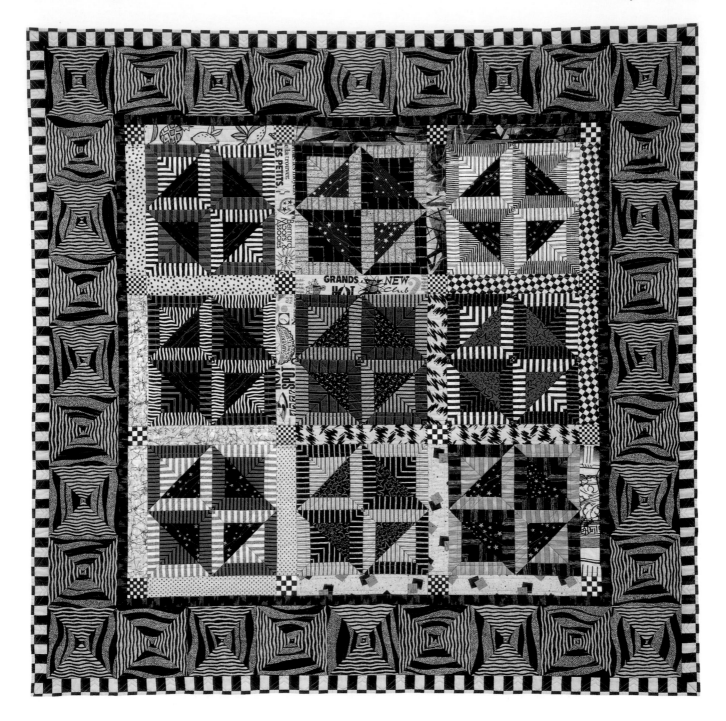

CHECKER CAB: NEW YORK CITY, 2 A.M.

COMMERCIAL AND HAND-SILKSCREENED (BY KATIE PASQUINI MASOPUST)
FABRICS; MACHINE PIECED AND MACHINE QUILTED; 64 x 64 INCHES.

*New York City fascinates me, and I wanted to make a story quilt that would capture an impression
of the place. On one trip I awoke at 2:00 A.M. and was amazed to hear the cacophony of sounds
outside my window . . . taxis and cars still going strong with their horns. I decided to work with this
sound memory.*

CALYX 2

COMMERCIAL COTTON; MACHINE PIECED AND HAND QUILTED WITH METALLIC
THREAD; 55 x 61 INCHES.

*Love of botany and quilting join forces in my Calyx series, a study of the outer floral envelope reduced
to its simplest elements. Cultivation of flowers in my garden and my quilt making process requires time
and care; I've learned patience from both.*

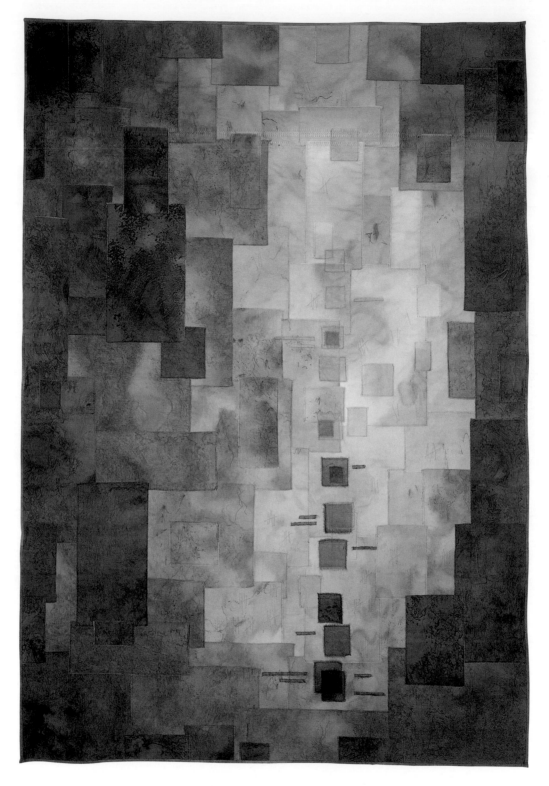

T RACES V

As a metaphor for time, the cave can be seen as both a timeless and a time-filled environment. On the
walls in Traces V are machine-stitched counting marks, reminiscent of marks scratched by a survivor.
The counting, however, becomes less accurate near the top of the quilt, challenging the meaning of
counting as it relates to time.

JUROR'S AWARD OF MERIT

REPEAT BLOCK IV: VESSELS

COTTON FABRIC EMBELLISHED WITH INK, ACRYLIC PAINT, AND COMPUTER
PROCESS; MACHINE PIECED, HAND AND MACHINE QUILTED; 29 x 25 INCHES.

*The world of postage stamps, with its array of multiple images and its abundance of borders and text, is
a rich source of inspiration for me. Also, I find the sampler and repeat block formats together irresistible
for their invitation to express "sameness within difference" and "difference within sameness." Repeat
Block IV: Vessels reflects my penchant for making the border an active part of my compositions and
for using the visual qualities of text.*

DESERT SKY

WOOL FABRIC EMBELLISHED WITH COUCHED WOOLEN YARNS; MACHINE PIECED
AND MACHINE QUILTED; 41 x 36 INCHES.

*Desert Sky was inspired by my memory of a camping trip in Central Australia many years ago.
Despite the rich, vast landscape, the land is still overwhelmed by the clear blue sky.*

QUILTS JAPAN PRIZE

TEA WILL MAKE IT BETTER

COMMERCIAL COTTON AND RAYON, FOUND TEXTILE OBJECTS; MACHINE PIECED,
HAND APPLIQUÉD, AND MACHINE QUILTED; 61 x 71 INCHES.

I did not drink tea at all when I first met my husband, but I finally yielded to his frequent offerings to have a cup. Over the years, tea has been a great source of enjoyment. Through both its delicious flavors and its ritualistic preparation, the experience of tea is a comfort. Whether faced with exhaustion, tension, confusion, anxiety, or cold, tea will make it better.

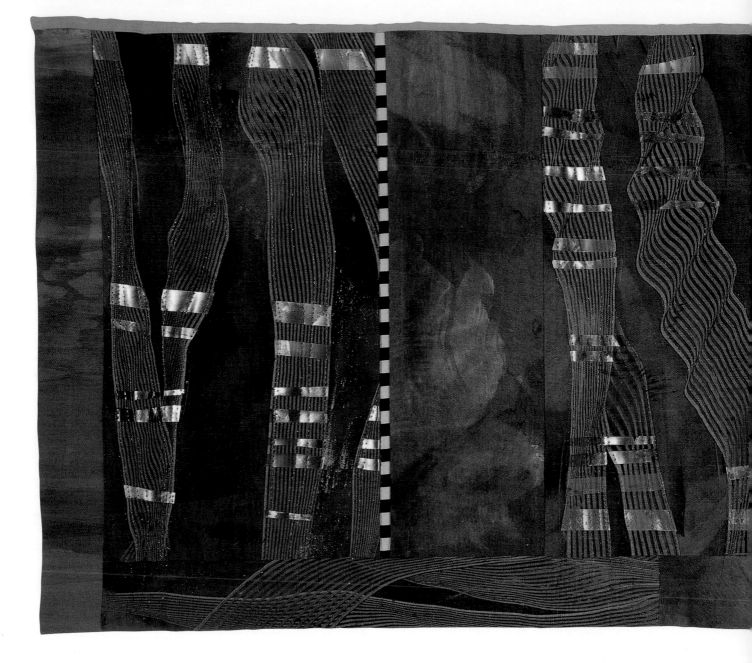

G R E A T   B A R R I E R   R E E F :   S U B M E R G E

TEXTILE INKS ON CANVAS, EMBELLISHED WITH ACETATE, METAL LEAF, AND MICA
POWDERS; MACHINE PIECED AND MACHINE QUILTED; 49 X 20 INCHES.

*This spring I had the good fortune to teach for several weeks in Australia. At the end of this time I spent
a day on the Great Barrier Reef. I was awestruck by the unreal color of both water and fish, and I
attempted to remember and put such color to canvas as soon as I returned to Maine.*

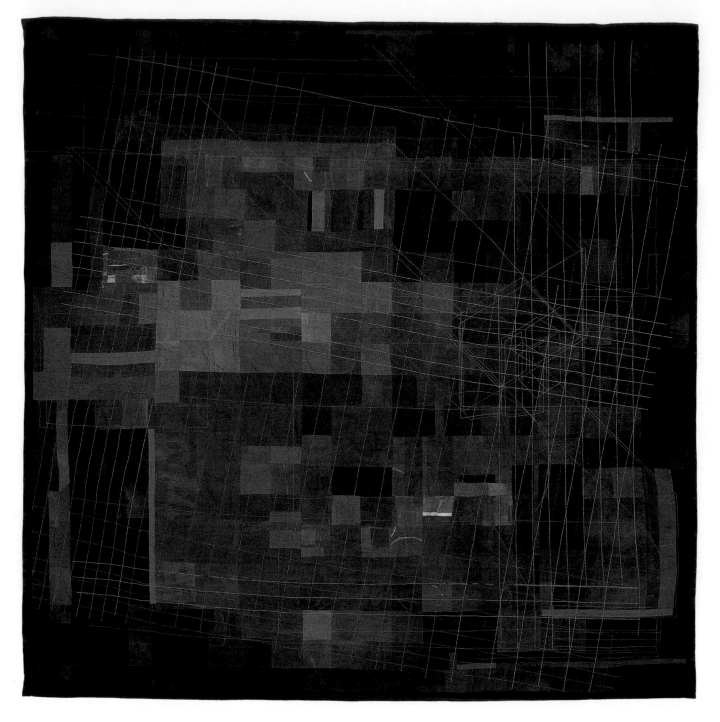

HOUSE AT ABIQUIU LAKE

HAND-DYED COTTON FABRICS; MACHINE PIECED AND EMBELLISHED WITH HAND
AND MACHINE TOPSTITCHING, MACHINE QUILTED; 52 x 52 INCHES.

*Years ago I regularly traveled back and forth between Albuquerque and Northern New Mexico to take
my children to their father's house at Abiquiu Lake. The experience translated into a blue field where
linear objects give reference to enclosure, while the composition alludes to dissolution of boundaries.
Superimposed and dissociated systems of stitched lines, pieced patterns, and bleached marks interface
and associate the urban grid of one world with the rural landscape of another.*

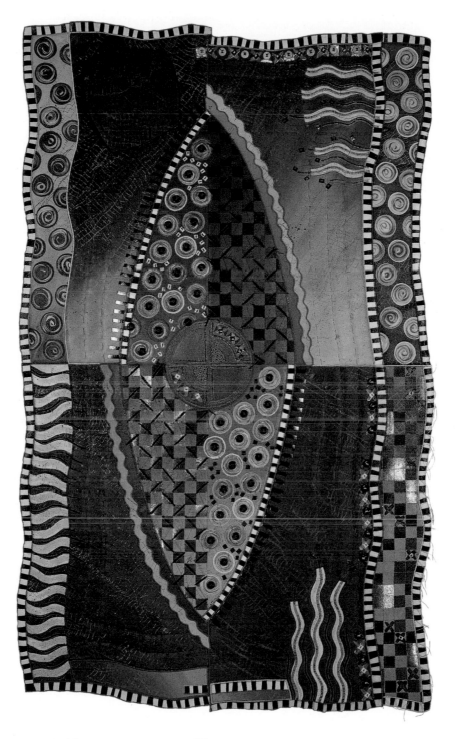

FOR THE TRIBE OF THE
ONE-BREASTED WOMEN

PAINTED COTTON CANVAS; MACHINE APPLIQUÉD AND COLLAGED, HAND AND
MACHINE QUILTED, EMBELLISHED WITH BUTTONS, BEADS, AND METALLIC FAB-
RICS; 37 X 60 INCHES.

An artist friend's courageous battle with breast cancer inspired a series of works entitled Shields
for Women Warriors. *The idea of soft armor that provided psychological protection with its positive
energy soon grew into a visual way to deal with my own realities: menopause, hot flashes, and a
mother with Alzheimer's.* For the Tribe of the One-Breasted Women *is for Lee and all heroic
souls surviving with humor and grace.*

S P R I N G

WOVEN FABRIC STRIPS; WOVEN IN SIX PARTS, ADHERED TO INTERFACING, THEN
WOVEN TOGETHER AND SEWN TO A BACKING; 52 x 77 INCHES.

For many years I have been exploring color progressions. I am fascinated by the way colors change each other as they move together in a sequence. Recently my work has involved smaller units combined to make larger forms. I model my work from music and growth patterns in nature.

VILLAGE STREET

COMMERCIAL COTTONS; MACHINE PIECED, HAND APPLIQUÉD, AND MACHINE QUILTED; 43 x 53 INCHES.

Currently I am using architectural themes developed mostly from memories of places visited and some never seen. Sometimes I record the exact delight I felt in a particular place; other times reality and fantasy mingle. By and large, all of my quilts reflect loves and interests, past and present.

TALLIT FOR MAURYCY GOTTLIEB

PHOTO SILKSCREENED SILK NOIL; MACHINE PIECED AND HAND QUILTED; 48 x 76 INCHES. FROM A PRIVATE COLLECTION.

This Jewish prayer shawl honors the 19th-century artist Gottlieb and his painting Jews Praying in the Synagogue on Yom Kippur. We made it as part of a protest against the Museum of the Diaspora in Tel Aviv, where an altered reproduction of the painting (the women looking on in the background were removed) was mounted. It was an outrage both to artists and women that required our reflection.

RAINBOW GARDEN — A GREEN QUILT

PAINTED CANVAS, FOUND OBJECTS AND MATERIALS, INCLUDING BOTTLE CAPS,
WOODEN SPOONS, AND CLOTHESPINS; HAND EMBROIDERED, HAND APPLIQUÉD,
AND HAND QUILTED; 94 x 78 INCHES. COURTESY MOBILIA GALLERY,
CAMBRIDGE, MASSACHUSETTS.

*This is our diary of the gardening season in our rainbow-shaped garden. We offer it as a healing bless-
ing for all gardens of the Earth, embodied in the central garden goddess, our Irish friend and artist,
Bridget O'Connell. Her pincushion harvest befits a quilter. The leather raccoons were caught together
(and freed) as we struggled to get rid of a groundhog. Sewn-in paintings on wood honor our cat, Vikki,
and the trapping of the groundhog.*

H O S T E S S   W I T H   T H E   M O S T E S T   I I

COMMERCIAL COTTONS AND BLENDS TREATED WITH IMMERSION DYEING,
DIRECT APPLICATION OF DYES AND PAINTS, AND STAMPING; MACHINE PIECED
AND MACHINE QUILTED; 70 x 45 INCHES.

The series began with a black and white cotton piqué print from the skirt of a 1970's floor-length hostess dress I rescued from a garage sale at my mother's house. My mother led me to fabric. She taught me to sew. She made me rip seams out and do them again. This quilt is a tribute to my mom, Joanne Benner, the hostess with the mostest.

TABOO

RECYCLED 100% SILK FABRIC; ENGLISH PAPER-PIECED, HAND QUILTED; 55 x 51 INCHES.

—

"Taboo," a Polynesian word for menstruation, also means sacred, valuable, magic, and frightening. It connotes immutable law and the forbidden, expressing recognition of the female origin of the power of blood. Using scraps of recycled clothing, I attempted to express an awareness of inner body/mind or "feeling tones" that otherwise are difficult to communicate.

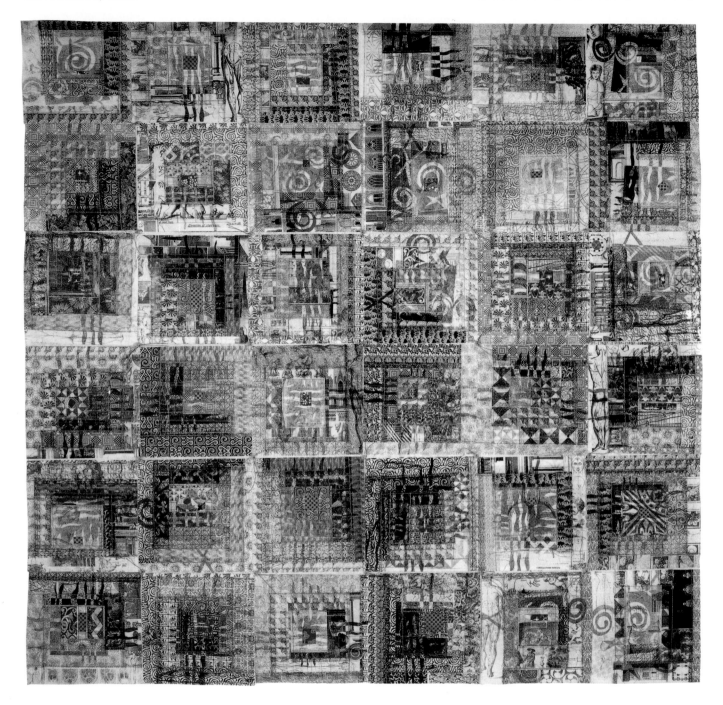

L O G C A B I N F O R
H I L D E G A R D V O N B I N G E N

PHOTOCOPIED AND HAND-PAINTED INTERFACING AND CLEAR TRANSPARENCIES;
FUSED, MACHINE AND HAND STITCHED, AND BEADED; 50 x 50 INCHES.

I like to listen to the music of Hildegard von Bingen, a 12th-century Christian mystic. It is ethereal, pure, and beautiful. I also like to interpret traditional designs in new materials. Industrial interfacing and imagery on transparencies are natural media to use as we speed toward the end of this century. Hildegard's Log Cabin cannot physically warm anyone, but it can be a visual "comforter" because it speaks of the wealth of human experience and diversity that precedes us, much as an old quilt comforts us with reminders of a familial past.

REGARD

COMMERCIAL AND HAND-DYED COTTONS, LAMÉ; MACHINE PIECED AND HAND QUILTED; 64 x 61 INCHES.

I started with my own photographs of a flower arrangement . . . precise images that became increasingly blurred. My aim, as I sewed the small blocks together, was to begin with a "destructured" image and end with a structured one. Why Regard? Because I wanted to lead the "spectator" to think about the meaning of my work. At first and from a distance, one would only see smooth outlines. With a closer viewing, one would see the jagged lines that simulate the look of live flowers.

BARBARA OLIVER HARTMAN

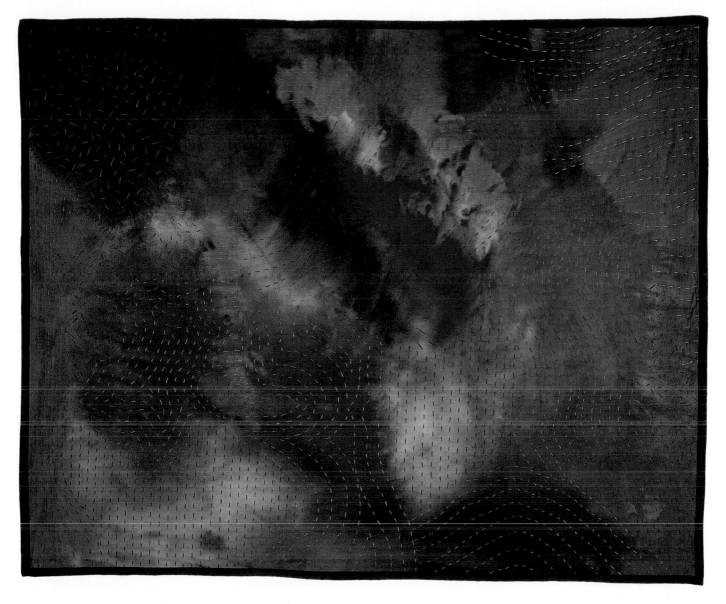

ATMOSPHERIC EVENT

DYE-PAINTED COTTON FABRIC; HAND STITCHED AND HAND QUILTED; 44 X 36 INCHES.

This quilt is part of an ongoing series about global warming. When an accident or emergency occurs at a nuclear power plant, the public is informed of an event. When atmospheric conditions reach critical stages, will they be described as events? We already have "Ozone Action Days."

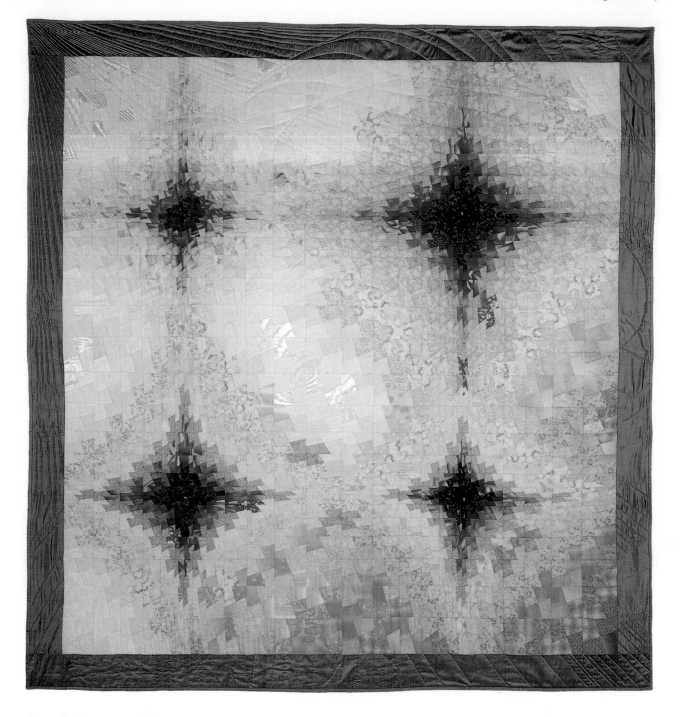

JUROR'S AWARD OF MERIT

A GUST OF WIND

COTTON, BLENDS, AND SILK FABRICS; HAND AND MACHINE PIECED, HAND QUILTED; 84 x 88 INCHES.

I like to create a sense of movement by using a variety of fabric piece sizes in my quilts. I always hope that people will think that the quilt tells a story.

W H A T N E X T ?

PHOTO SILKSCREENED, STENCILLED, OVERDYED, AND COMMERCIAL COTTONS;
MACHINE PIECED, HAND APPLIQUÉD, AND HAND QUILTED; 38 x 74 INCHES.

I'm still playing with language and layering. After Boris Yeltsin won the July, 1996 presidential election, the Russian newspaper Izvestia ran the headline "Democracy Wins / What Next?" Having been in Russia a few months earlier, that phrase had a certain resonance for me. I hope this quilt — despite its surreal, floating shapes — captures some of the color and feel of Moscow.

INTERSECTIONS #5

COTTONS, HAND-DYED FABRICS (BY MICHELE DUELL), SOME EMBELLISHED WITH
ACRYLIC PAINT; MACHINE PIECED AND MACHINE QUILTED; 57 x 58 INCHES.

*Intersections are where the action is, where two lines cross, where streets cross, where things overlap.
Intersections are symbolic of connection. In some cases, though, such as where two wide, busy streets
cross, intersections can be alienating. For me, the symbolic meaning enriches work that can be enjoyed
on purely visual terms.*

ROOKIE AWARD

S H A D O W

NEEDLEPOINT PANELS WITH THREAD AND FABRIC COLLAGE; MACHINE
APPLIQUÉD AND MACHINE QUILTED; 37 x 37 INCHES.

My quilts mark the path of a spiritual journey. The images come from dreams and are influenced by research into their symbolic messages. The fish, which is often in my dreams, is thought to act as a guide to the unconscious because it never closes its eyes. As such, it inspired a series of pieces that acknowledge and honor a part of my nature that is wild, mysterious, and filled with potential.

BARE ROOT

COMMERCIAL AND HAND-DYED COTTON FABRICS; MACHINE PIECED AND
MACHINE QUILTED; 61 X 37 INCHES.

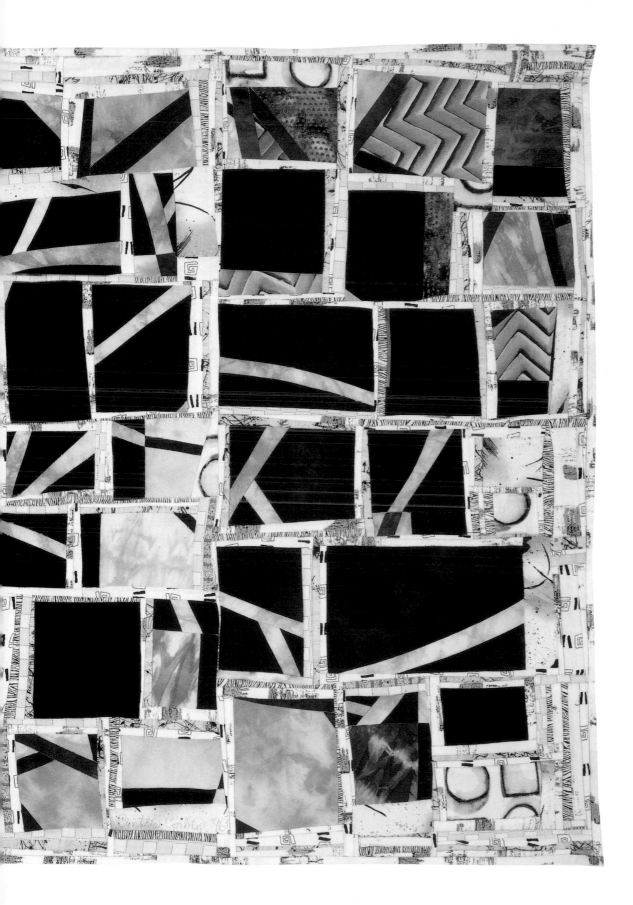

I am interested in abstract images and the expression of something intangible through this medium of fabric. This is my language. My quilts are my poems. They allow me to say something.

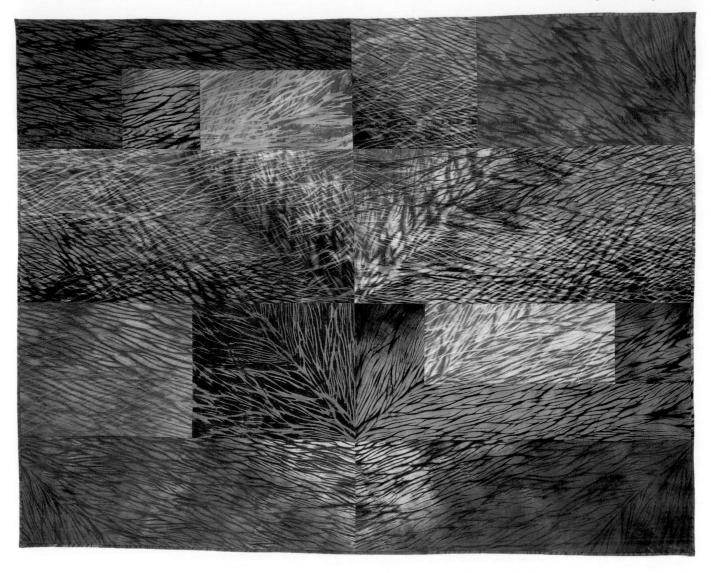

THE TRYSTING TREE

COTTON MUSLIN THAT HAS BEEN TIED, DYED AND (SOMETIMES) BLEACHED;
MACHINE PIECED AND MACHINE QUILTED; 76 X 58 INCHES.

I love creating these fabrics — layering color on color, then removing some. I love the way depth and light saturate each individual piece. I cut them as little as necessary . . . the fabrics themselves are so evocative that the challenge for me is to hear their message and combine them in ways that increase their strength and beauty. The title refers to an image from the novel Snow Falling on Cedars.

D R A I N S   A N D   F A L L I N G   W A T E R S

SAMPLES OF COTTON DECORATOR FABRICS AND PHOTO TRANSFERS; PIECED
AND HAND QUILTED; 20 x 20 INCHES.

The use of the photo transfer technique is just another way to enhance fabric with surface design. The photographs of the drains and pond were taken on the grounds of the Pontifical College Josephinum while attending the Quilt Surface Design Symposium in Columbus, Ohio. The Falling Waters photograph was taken years earlier on the grounds of the famous house in Pennsylvania by Frank Lloyd Wright. It seemed appropriate to combine the two into this simple nine-patch quilt.

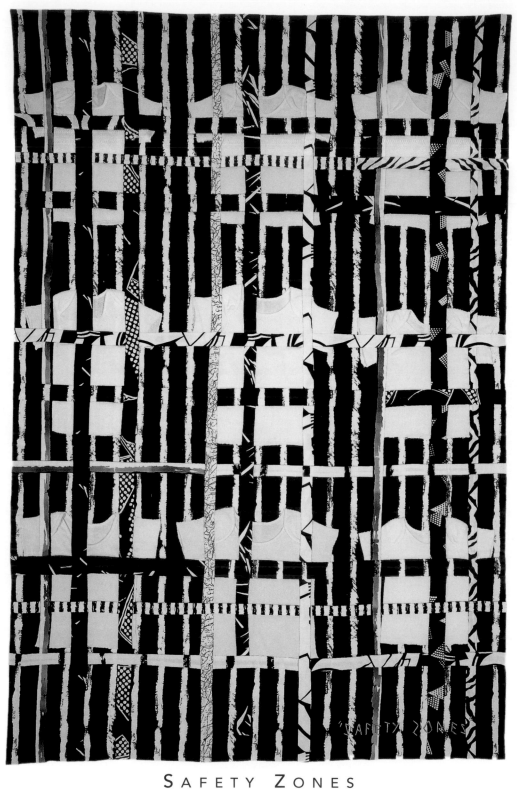

SAFETY ZONES

COMMERCIAL FABRICS AND USED INFANT T-SHIRTS; HAND APPLIQUÉD TO A
WHOLE CLOTH BACKGROUND; 42 x 63 INCHES.

I have strong concerns about the issue of child abuse. Safety Zones is part of a series which uses the generic imagery of the infant shirt to explore issues of vulnerability and protection. My desire to symbolically hold and secure our children by "weaving" them into the protective surface of the quilt is expressed in Safety Zones. Paradoxically, however, such restrictive protection often stunts children's emotional development. Perhaps Safety Zones? would be a better title.

SHARON HEIDINGSFELDER

FRIENDS ON THE OTHER SIDE

COTTON FABRICS, SOME SILKSCREENED BY THE ARTIST; MACHINE PIECED AND
MACHINE QUILTED; 46 x 49 INCHES.

So you think everything that happens to you is of your own making?

1 - 2 - 3 - 4

COTTONS AND SILKS; MACHINE APPLIQUÉD AND MACHINE QUILTED;
54 x 66 INCHES.

*Beat. 1-2-3-4. Shadows, crooked lines, a reflection. Beat. Something added, a change. The balancing
act doesn't stop. Life, it throws you a curve. Take the next step. Beat.*

AWARD OF EXCELLENCE

AGED: COVERED BY WISDOM

FABRIC, CONSTRUCTION BOARD, PIECES OF PINE; HAND STITCHED AND TIED;
108 x 108 INCHES.

Time and nurturing are carried through rings of wisdom. These rings are displayed in their natural form through geometric cuts. The patterns allow the viewer to visualize the existence and environmental history of this tree and how it has sheltered and nurtured the earth.

WIFE WANTED

VARIOUS FABRICS EMBELLISHED WITH STENCILS, T-SHIRT TRANSFERS, SCREEN-
PRINTING, AND AIRBRUSHED PAINT; MACHINE QUILTED; 67 X 47 INCHES.

I found this ad in a magazine from the 1940s. "Wife Wanted: Must be graduate engineer in electronics. Preferably checked out on jet bomber controls. Sardine packing experience valuable. Should be accomplished contortionist." To me this clearly states the talents women possess.

UNTITLED

COTTON, WOOL, SILK, AND BLENDED FABRICS; FUSED, APPLIQUÉD, EMBROI-
DERED, AND QUILTED; 50 x 48 INCHES.

Of all the really bad things that can happen to you, making a mistake with a piece of fabric is not one. This perspective — newly acquired as a result of a 1993 breast cancer diagnosis — allowed me to do such things as cut into expensive fabric without having a plan, leave edges unfinished and raw, and defiantly stitch "outside the lines," reflecting both the truly awful times and the wonderful new freedoms.

R E L I Q U A R Y

TRITIK-DISCHARGED COTTON TREATED WITH WAX RESIST, DYES AND
PEARLESCENT PAINTS APPLIED WITH STAMPS; HAND AND MACHINE STITCHED,
AND EMBELLISHED WITH BEADS, CORDS, AND CHARMS; 52 x 48 INCHES.
FROM A PRIVATE COLLECTION.

Making Reliquary involved many basic techniques of manipulating fabric, some dating back thousands of years and most traditionally performed by women. For me, the piece brings to mind relics sometimes seen in Italian cathedrals: a bit of some saint's shroud, a lock of another saint's hair. I wanted to create the feeling of a small chapel in a large cathedral: ancient and rich, mysterious, and quiet.

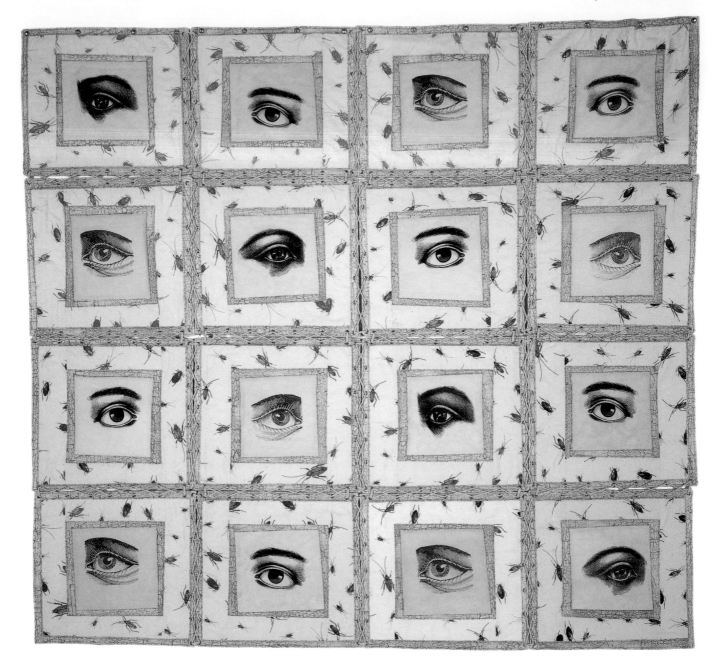

WE'RE NEVER REALLY ALONE...

COMMERCIAL FABRICS AS WELL AS OTHERS CREATED THROUGH COLOR XEROGRAPHY AND LITHOGRAPHY; MACHINE PIECED AND QUILTED; LACED WITH COTTON YARN THROUGH BRASS EYELETS; 48 X 50 INCHES.

Are we ever really alone? Life takes many forms. What about your religious beliefs? Do you believe in ghosts? And in this obsessed, techno-saturated society of World Wide Webs, cellular phones, televisions, and video cameras, how can we be alone? Whether we like it or not, we're all connected. So then...is "alone" more a mental than a physical state of being? Well, I'll leave you alone with your thoughts now... or maybe not...

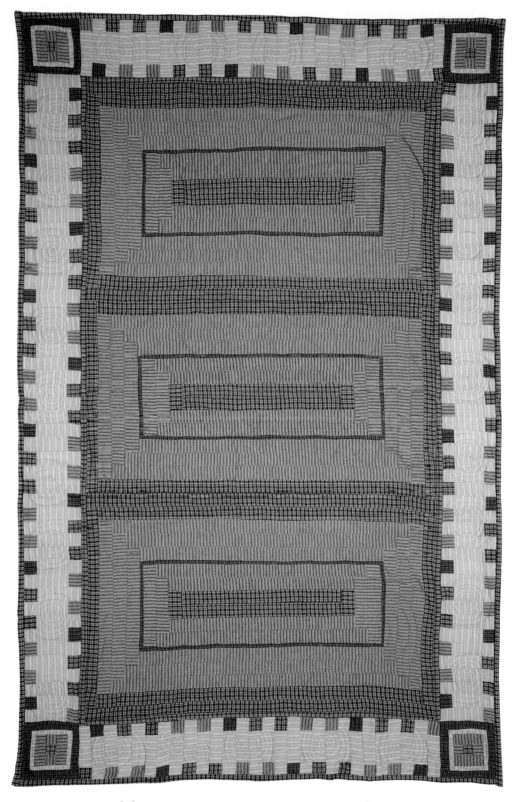

METAPHOR FOR A BED

COMMERCIAL FABRICS; MACHINE PIECED AND MACHINE QUILTED; 44 x 70 INCHES.

I started making quilts because I love combining two disparate things — old and new, traditional and contemporary, staid and quirky. In this quilt I took the traditional log cabin block, skewed it into huge rectangles (using old fashioned fabrics), and added an old-timey pieced border. Then I started freestyle quilting in fanciful, fun spirals and squiggles.

L I N E N   C L O S E T

SILK, COTTON, NYLON NET, AND LINEN EMBELLISHED WITH ACRYLIC AND TEXTILE
PAINTS; HAND APPLIQUÉD, EMBROIDERED, AND HAND QUILTED; 29 X 65 INCHES.

*When I was young, I would go to the end of the hall and open the mirrored door to the linen closet. As
I approached with the week's clean towels and sheets, my reflection would usher me in. Here's a place
where the fabrics, usually intimate and functional in our lives, are neither. The linen closet is layers
of folds and shadows, softness and textures, surprises of color, all contrasted against hard, narrow strips
of shelves.*

THE SOUTHERN MOON

HAND-DYED AND HAND-BATIKED COTTON FABRIC; MACHINE PIECED AND HAND
QUILTED; 51 X 51 INCHES.

To fully experience and understand the world is to find patterns and relationships that are unique, while still being identifiable and repeatable. To make art is to do this with an object as evidence of the search. Below the surface of conscious seeing, art may speak specifically about what is universal, just as the inexactitude of a quilt may be masked to suggest an energy that cannot be calculated.

CHINESE TILES

SEMI-TRANSPARENT RIBBON FOLDED AND ENCASED IN PLASTIC; MACHINE
STITCHED AND HAND TIED; 44 x 54 INCHES.

*Unlike most quilts, this quilt emphasizes the inner layer. Both sides of the quilt are transparent, allow-
ing the colorful inner layer to show. Changing the background color, which also shows through the quilt,
alters the viewer's reaction to the quilt.*

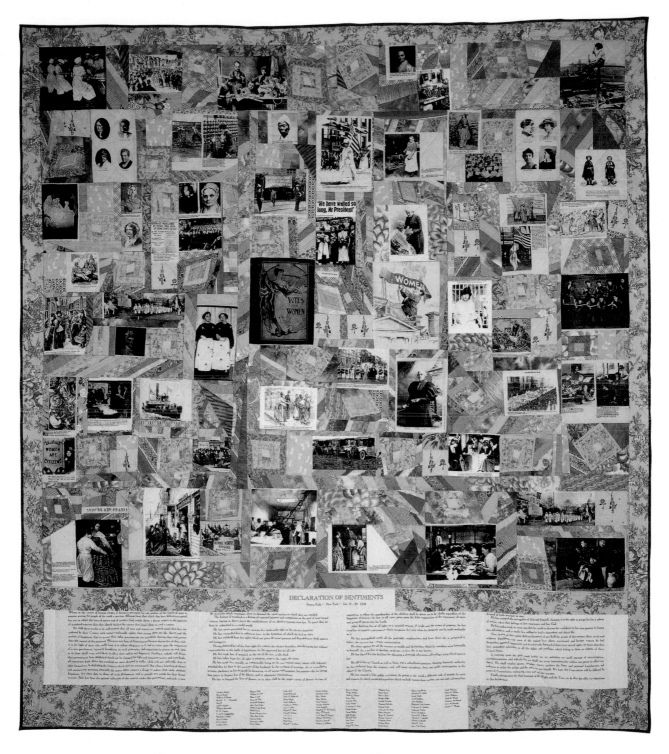

RESISTANCE TO TYRANNY IS
OBEDIENCE TO GOD

COTTON, SILK, VINTAGE AMERICAN FABRICS FROM THE MID-1800S THROUGH THE 1920S, PHOTO TRANSFERS; MACHINE PIECED AND QUILTED; 71 x 79 INCHES.

This quilt celebrates the 75th anniversary of women's suffrage. It illuminates and pays homage to the suffrage movement in America from its beginnings in 1848 to its passage in Congress in 1920. With historical photos and images, vintage fabrics, and the full text of the Declaration of Sentiments, I wanted this quilt to be a testament to the people who fulfilled Susan B. Anthony's statement, "Resistance to Tyranny is obedience to God."

YVONNE FORMAN

Hastings-on-Hudson, New York

JUROR'S AWARD OF MERIT

EINSTEIN & TOMATOES

COTTON FABRIC AND LASER PRINTER PHOTO TRANSFERS; MACHINE PIECED AND
HAND QUILTED (BY GRACE MILLER); 41 x 41 INCHES.

—

Einstein & Tomatoes reflects my continued fascination with geometry, found objects, nontraditional art materials, and the transformation that occurs when an ordinary object is placed in an unexpected context. In this piece I juxtapose the high-tech, laser-printed photo transfer with the traditional nine-patch block, dissolving boundaries and reordering fragments in pursuit of what can happen when two unlikely elements meet.

I K O N

COTTON FABRICS; MACHINE PIECED AND MACHINE QUILTED; 74 x 79 INCHES.

This quilt was motivated in part by a desire to simplify, to return to elemental forms and relationships, and was inspired by a 15th-century Russian icon.

B U R N T   P I N E   F O R E S T   # 3

COTTON PHOTOCOPY TRANSFERS CUT AND FUSED OR STITCHED TO COTTON
FABRIC; MACHINE QUILTED; 56 X 42 INCHES.

In June, 1995, eight years after the Yellowstone fire, I expected to be saddened by the sight of the vast
burned forest. I thought it would look like a commercial clear-cut forest, ravaged and raw, exposed. But
far from being ugly or boring scenery, the burned area appeared to be part of the forest's natural life
cycle. Perfectly formed little pine trees grew abundantly amidst the still-standing timber "snags" and
fallen branches. The contrast between the blue sky, blackened trees, and lush green forest floor was
striking and unexpected.

A T   T H E   P O N D

SINGLE-USE STENCIL ON SPONGE-PRINTED FABRIC; TRAPUNTO, HAND EMBROI-
DERY, HAND QUILTING; 20 x 56 INCHES.

STREETDANCE

HAND-DYED COTTON; FUSED AND MACHINE QUILTED; 69 x 51 INCHES.

Strolling on an upstate New York campus last summer, I thought I saw a figure formed by the cracks in the sidewalk under my feet. I photographed the pavement and later began a series of quilts based on those intriguing cracks. I love the way the cracked line is sustained from block to block as it deteriorates. My contribution was to change the color from utilitarian concrete gray to the vibrant colors of the fiesta.

A P RAYER FOR S YLVAIN

H AND-DYED AND/OR PAINTED COTTON FABRICS; MACHINE PIECED AND
MACHINE QUILTED; 35 x 42 INCHES.

This quilt is part of a series about my relationship with a dear friend who died of AIDS in May of
1995. When I first heard of Sylvain's illness, I was so frightened about what would happen to him and
to his partner, John. I had horrible nightmares, waking up terrified every morning, as though I were on
the brink of death myself. I said many prayers for Sylvain, hoping somehow to make life easier, and
hoping he knew I cared.

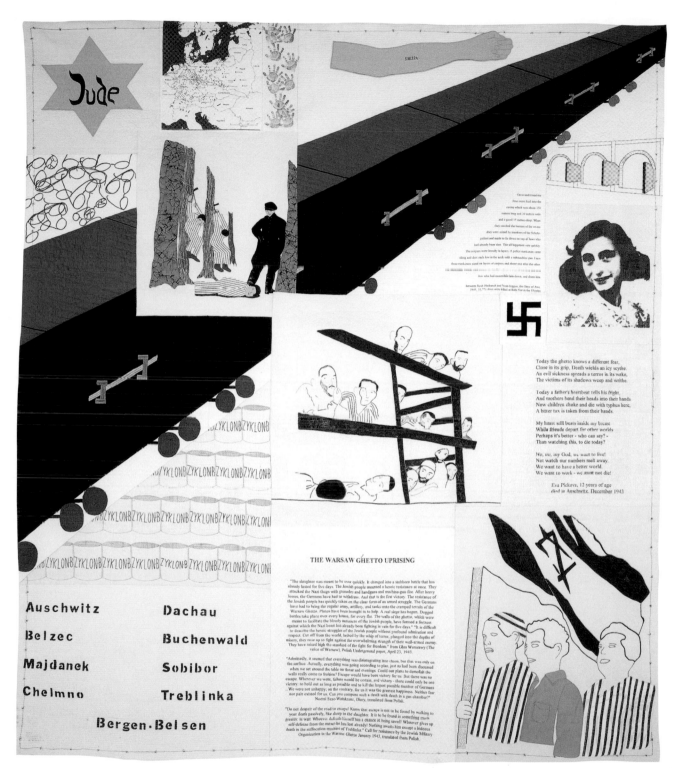

LEST WE FORGET

COTTON FABRIC THAT HAS BEEN STAMPED, PAINTED, STENCILLED, AND EMBELLISHED WITH HEAT TRANSFERS; MACHINE PIECED, MACHINE APPLIQUED, MACHINE EMBROIDERED, AND MACHINE QUILTED; 67 x 77 INCHES.

This work expresses my feelings about the Holocaust as we pass the 50th anniversary of the liberation of the camps. After visiting Yad Vashem, the Holocaust museum in Israel, I had to express these feelings. It is a tribute to those who died and to those who continue to die because of prejudice. Notice that the swastika is not quilted into the quilt.

S N O W

COTTON, SILK, AND WOOL FABRICS EMBELLISHED WITH ACRYLIC PAINT; MACHINE
PIECED AND HAND QUILTED; 89 X 46 INCHES.

In snow, shapes and patterns become abstractly detached and isolated by the delicately wind-chiseled drifting snow. Billowing snowfall in rapidly changing descents has designs and rhythms of rich luxuriance; the airy weightlessness of massing clumps, the smooth gliding of sharp, perfect flakes, the rapid descent of heavy snow drops.

PSYCHO MOMS BAKE A CAKE

COMMERCIAL COTTON, VINTAGE FABRICS, AND OLD CLOTHING; HAND AND
MACHINE PIECED, EMBROIDERED, STAMPED, APPLIQUÉD, AND HAND QUILTED
(BY KATHERINE McKEARN); 81 x 77 INCHES.

This is it.

L O O K I N G F O R G O D

PAINTED CANVAS EMBELLISHED WITH BEADS, BUTTONS, SEQUINS, AND FOUND
OBJECTS; HAND STITCHED AND TIED; 64 x 74 INCHES.

I wanted to do a quilt about my black lab, Barker, who was my studio companion for 13 years. I've sketched and pondered and dreamed on this for several years. While finishing a name quilt of historical Kentucky women, I thought of a name quilt using dog names. What finally came together was a background for another quilt I'd started called Looking for God (for which I could not find the central image), the dog names I had collected, and a desire to bead this dog head. The dog is my current lab, Belle. I couldn't imagine beading the body too; thus the dress. My husband asks, "Why the potholder?" It represents the unknown. I had fun, fun, fun making this quilt. I even said aloud, "I don't care if anyone likes this quilt; I like it." I kept the title because of what "God" spells backward.

MOZZIES: DON'T YOU JUST HATE 'EM!

TEXTILE INKS APPLIED TO COTTON FABRIC; MACHINE PIECED AND MACHINE QUILTED; 41 x 41 INCHES.

It's late at night and your body craves sleep. You lie still in the darkness. Suddenly, you hear a whining noise and before you know it you are up on the bed, trying to smash that sound through the ceiling!

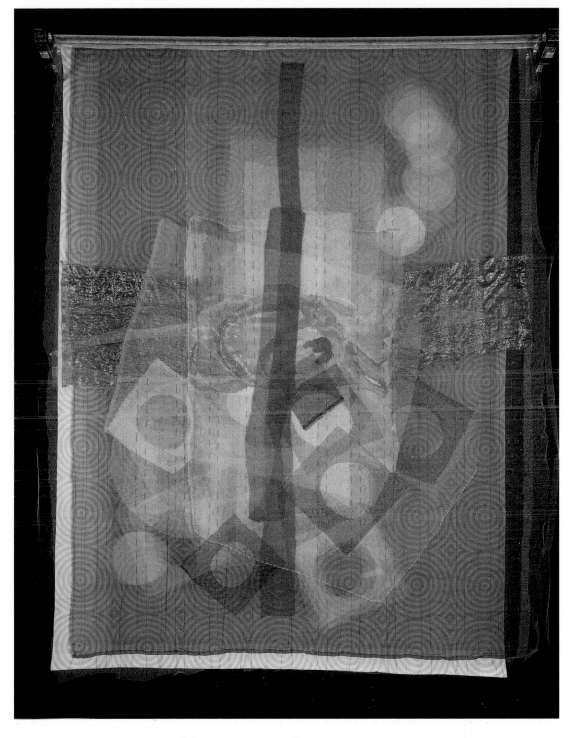

VEILED SUNRISE

FOREGROUND PIECE: SILK AND POLYESTER ORGANZA, HAND-DYED SILK CHIFFON, NETTING; HAND QUILTED WITH "SILVER" AND OTHER THREADS. BACKGROUND PIECE: COTTON FABRIC; HAND QUILTED WITH PEARL COTTON THREAD. 42 x 58 INCHES.

Each morning I watch the sun emerge through a veil of trees, sometimes shrouded by fog or rain. The squares and circles represent the splitting atom releasing its energy and dissipating into forces not so readily seen as in this special time of day. The circles on the backdrop heighten the sense of energy, and depending on the light source, shadows are cast from the foreground to the background, subtly demonstrating the presence of a power source.

LAKE SUPERIOR STICK BED

ASSORTED FABRICS; HAND APPLIQUÉD, HAND EMBROIDERED, HAND QUILTED
(BY SUE RULE), BEADED, AND EMBELLISHED WITH PAINT. THE BED WAS
DECOUPAGED WITH FABRIC, PAINT, AND STICKS. QUILT: 64 x 78 INCHES.
BED: 80 x 45 x 42.

I gathered these sticks while walking the shore of Lake Superior, thinking about pollution and our water system. We have come dangerously close to destroying our home, the planet Earth. This bed (with the wolves peering out behind the sticks) represents the environmental bed we have made, and now must sleep in.

SUMMER'S END

COTTON, LINEN, AND SILK; MACHINE PIECED AND STITCHED TO MUSLIN BACK-
ING, MOUNTED ON HIDDEN FRAME; 67 x 48 INCHES.

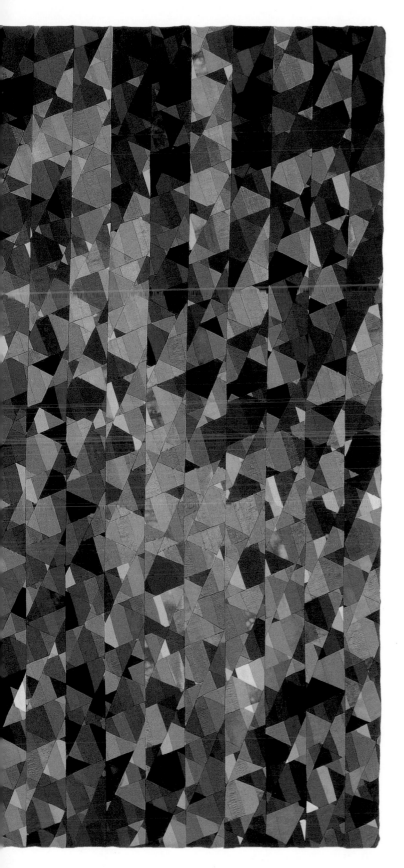

Summer's End is a response to the brilliance of color seen in gardens and landscapes around the country at the end of summer. The light at that time of year is just beginning to take on the intensity and clarity that comes in autumn, and all color seems especially vivid. Since the focus of my work is color and the continued development of a piecing process that allows color and fabric to be used in a free, painterly manner, I enjoy the drama of seasonal change.

85

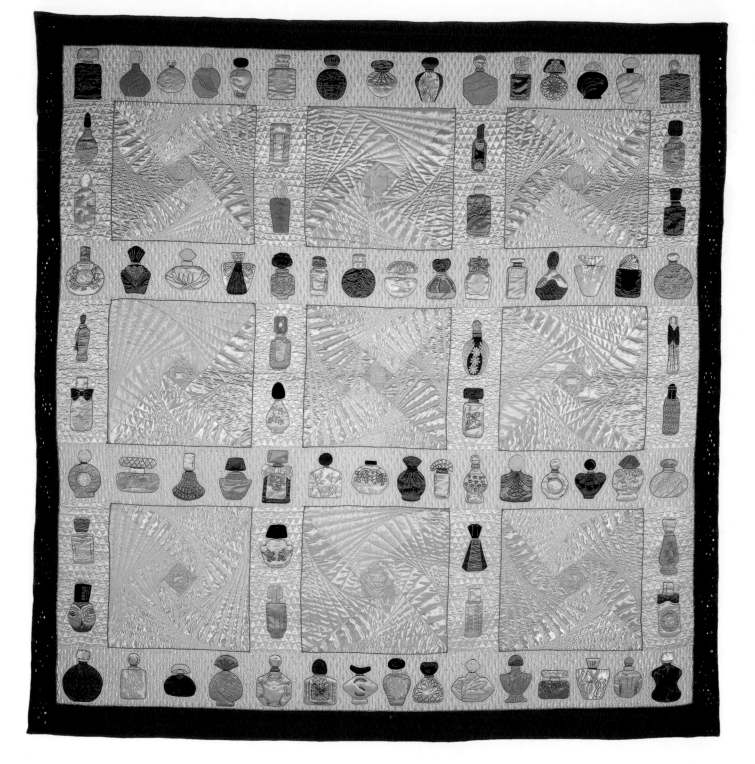

PERFUME

VARIOUS FABRICS EMBELLISHED WITH BUTTONS AND LACE; PIECED, APPLIQUÉD,
SMOCKED, AND HAND QUILTED; 81 x 82 INCHES.

I used luminous fabrics to express the mysterious scent and beautiful transparent colors of charming
perfume bottles. Cording enhances the sense of perspective in the center of the work and the pearl buttons in the smocked border give the work a wonderful visual appeal.

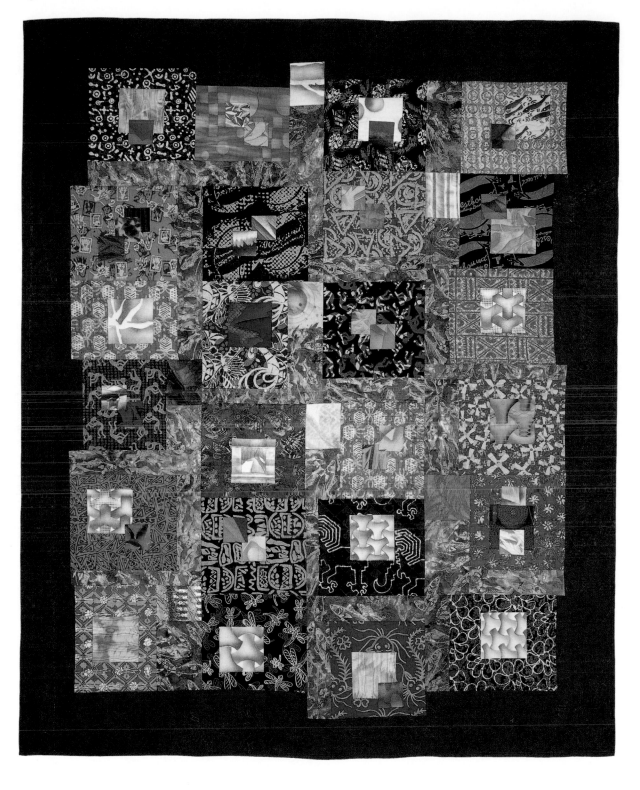

EXPLORING BALI

BALI BATIKS AND AIRBRUSHED COTTONS; MACHINE PIECED AND MACHINE QUILTED; 58 x 70 INCHES.

I put a selection of Bali batiks on my design wall to admire, and without my conscious involvement, a nearby pile of airbrushed samples migrated to the wall. They formed small abstract pictures within batik frames. Tradition became a frame for the future. The quilting enhances the contrast between the fabrics without competing for attention. The fabrics are the quilt.

EARTH SERIES — ICE

COMMERCIAL COTTON AND LAMÉ FABRICS; MACHINE PIECED AND MACHINE
QUILTED WITH RAYON, METALLIC, AND COTTON THREADS; 63 x 51 INCHES.

The Earth series exemplified my deep appreciation of the gifts the Earth continues to give me. These quilts are impressionist reminders, made as memorials of my favorite places and the Earth's bounty. Ice illustrates my love of the snow. I love the knowledge that I will be warm in the cold. I love to see the variety of colors reflected in the crystal flakes. I seek the contrast in the seemingly low-contrast landscapes. I love to ski in the quiet solitude of the big mountain landscape.

WINDMILL

HAND-DYED AND/OR DYE-PAINTED COMMERCIAL COTTON FABRICS; HAND AND
MACHINE PIECED, HAND AND MACHINE QUILTED; 76 X 81 INCHES.

Windmill *tells stories about both the Midwest, where I have strong roots, and the Southwest, where I now live. It tells of Don Quixote's obsession. It's the wheel of fortune, the roulette wheel, the wheel of life. Windmill is from my series of quilts about machinery. Machines both enable and handicap by giving us the ability to work alone. The elegant shapes in obsolete machinery often remind me of the human figure.*

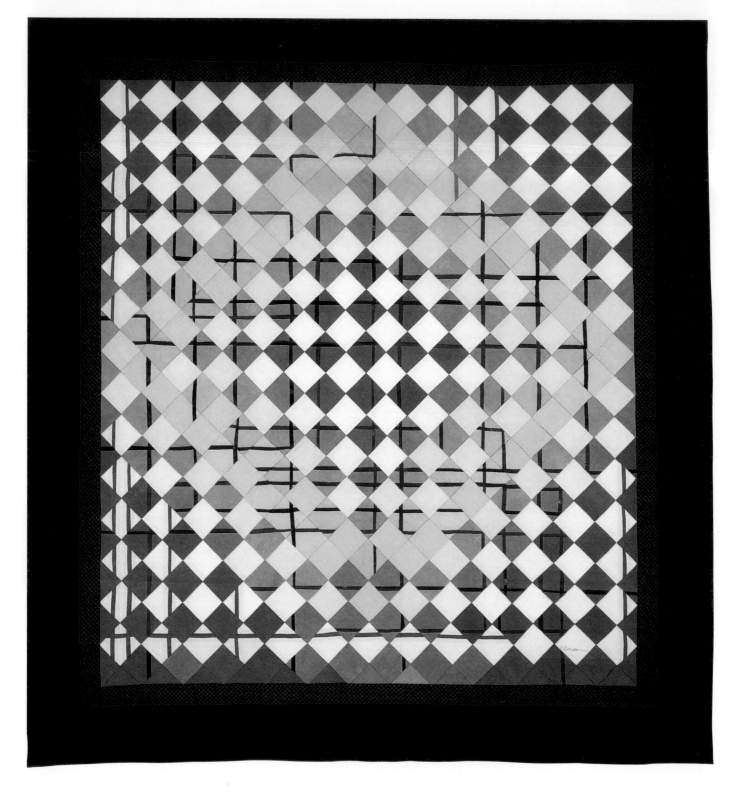

PLANE DREAMS

COMMERCIAL AND HAND-DYED COTTON; MACHINE PIECED AND QUILTED,
EMBELLISHED WITH EMBROIDERY FLOSS; 46 x 50 INCHES.

This piece is part of a series exploring space and dimension. It draws the viewer into a space beyond the surface with lights to beckon and mark the way. This quilt is dedicated to my grandfather, an inventor, who never faltered in his disciplined and enthusiastic search for knowledge and his quest for his dreams.

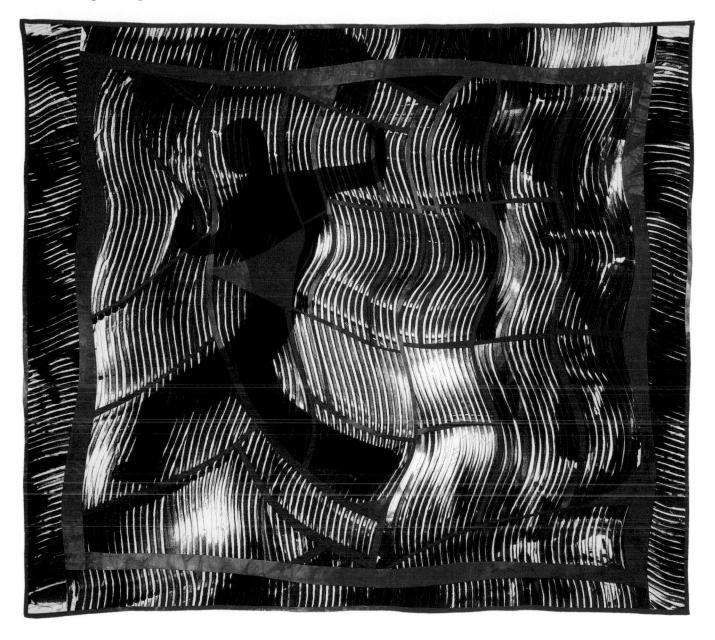

SHOCK WAVES

HAND-DYED COTTONS; MACHINE PIECED AND MACHINE QUILTED; 47 X
41 INCHES.

*Shock Waves came from the images embedded (accidentally) in the fabric I dyed. When I cut, pieced,
quilted, and dyed the fabric again, I did have a specific idea in mind, but I do not want to limit the
meanings of them by defining them. I enjoy knowing that my work may mean something very different
to viewers, and I regret that I do not hear their interpretations more often.*

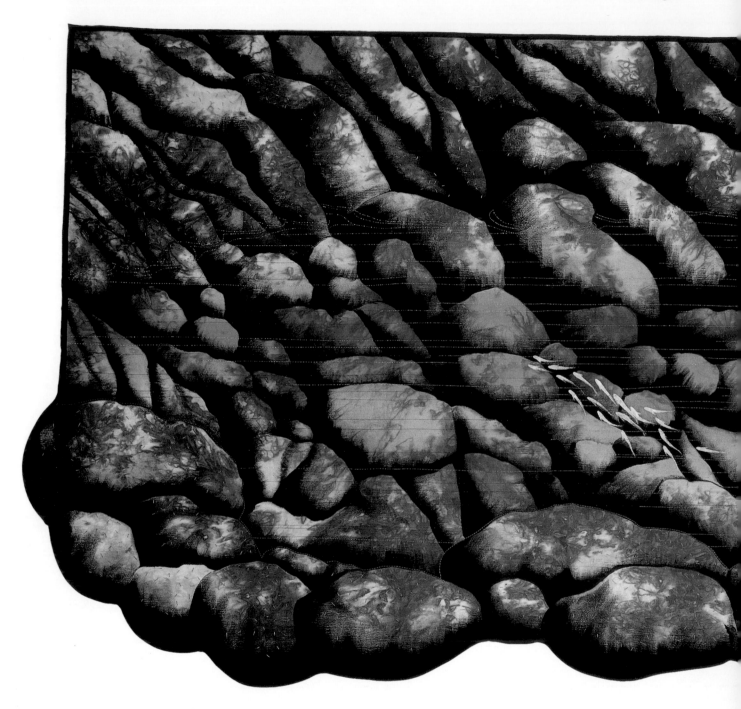

POOL

COTTON FABRIC TREATED WITH PROCION DYE AND METALLIC PIGMENT; HAND
AND MACHINE QUILTED; 56 X 31 INCHES.

This imaginary view of a quiet pool seems a bit strange and mysterious. The interface between air and water is obscure — where does one end and the other begin? The ideal pool of cool, clear, clean water, filled with life, is shown in an almost surreal setting. It is a contrast to reality. It is a dream.

INSIDE/OUT: CHAIRS

COTTON FABRICS HAND-DYED USING VARIATIONS OF SHIBORI TECHNIQUES;
MACHINE PIECED AND QUILTED; 38 x 29 INCHES.

Peake's Island, Maine. A memory of time at the shore where everything is change — tides, light, life, even rocks . . . marking time by the minute and the millennium. Now frozen in shape and line, pattern and color, a breathing space is recreated with layers of meaning both universal and personal. The organic pattern of shibori led my art to the coast!

CONSTELLATION II OR
THE DRESSMAKER'S WORKSHOP

COMMERCIAL FABRICS AND CLOTHING REMNANTS; HAND AND MACHINE
STITCHED AND QUILTED; 43 x 59 INCHES.

The French Larousse Encyclopedia *defines a constellation as a group of scattered objects on a
limited space. This quilt is a poetic reminder of the sky and the earth, of the astral influence the stars
have on human life. The background and foreground elements serve as a link between the two worlds.
I included the old apron as a way to honor the humble work of the hands that created the gardens and
crafts of the old days.*

TRIPTYCH: SOME LIKE IT HOT

COMMERCIAL AND HAND-PAINTED COTTONS AND RIBBON; MACHINE PIECED,
MACHINE APPLIQUÉD, AND HAND-QUILTED; 40 X 33 INCHES.

Some Like It Hot is a kitchen triptych: a household altar recalling the comfort and coziness of flow-
ered tablecloths, pots of tea, and curls of steam that warm a room.

BREAD; STAPLE, FOURTH REMOVED

HAND-DYED FABRICS PRINTED AND EMBELLISHED WITH TEXTILE PAINT; HAND
APPLIQUÉD, HAND PIECED, AND HAND QUILTED; 62 x 50 INCHES.

In some cultures, it is considered a breach of natural law to harm a person with whom one has broken bread.

FOREST CLOTH ONE

SILK FRAGMENTS; MACHINE-STITCHED TO RAYON/SILK VELVET AND HAND-DYED
RAYON VISCOSE TWILL, PAINTED WITH WATERBASED POLYURETHENE AND POLY-
ACRYLIC; 56 x 36 INCHES.

Forest Cloth One *maps connections between art and place. Silk fragments were hidden in tree hollows, creeks, and crevices of the forest for eight months to collect the marks of their place. Stained by maple innards, soil fungus, and creek algae, the fragments bear the effects of their site. The stitches suggest topography, perhaps the contours of the plateau from which it was created. Strata constructed of contrasting surfaces honors the significance of place to the process of creating.*

BEYOND THE BARS II

HAND-DYED COTTON; DIRECT APPLIQUÉD; MACHINE STITCHED AND MACHINE
QUILTED; 44 x 56 INCHES.

Bars: a metaphor for personal and social barriers. Curiosity: a fundamental aspect of the human mind.
Curiosity encourages us to cross barriers, to find what is hidden by the barrier. Occasionally we are sat-
isfied with our findings, but sometimes we are left frustrated. The urge to cross barriers, to explore the
other side, is mixed with fear of failure. Is it safer to stay on the known side?

SMOKE VEIL

COMMERCIAL AND HAND-DYED COTTON FABRICS; MACHINE PIECED,
DISCHARGED, SLASHED, AND HAND QUILTED; 42 x 53 INCHES.

*Like the black wedding veil worn on the Palestinian bride's symbolic journey to her husband's home and
her new life, bush fires signify not only the end of life, but also regrowth and new beginnings.*

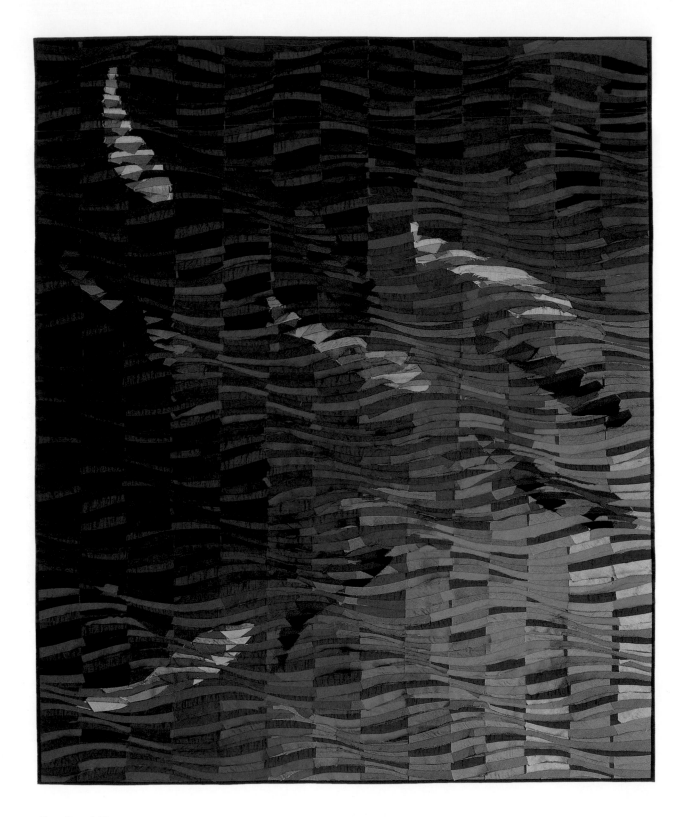

Two-Panel Piece

KOI DIPTYCH

THREE LAYERS OF SILK ON TWO COTTON BACKING LAYERS; REVERSE APPLIQUÉD
(STITCHING, CUTTING, AND PRESSING BY SHAWN BEHRENDS); 88 X 52 INCHES.

I wanted to create the illusion of depth and movement, to capture the way goldfish appear to flicker through the moving, reflective surface of water. Silk has the reflective quality of water. Reverse appliqué helps to create depth through contrast between layers. The offset wavy-line quilting and cutting create an illusion of wave motion. Composition and placement of fish between layers gives depth and motion. The specific cutting and pressing within the fish helps create the flickering quality.

ATTACHMENTS

COTTON, BLENDS, AND RAYON FABRICS, RIC-RAC, SEQUINS, METALLIC THREAD, BUT-
TONS, AND BRASS FITTINGS; STITCHED BY HAND AND MACHINE; 70 x 88 INCHES.

This is an enterprise of elements collected over a long period. Pockets salvaged from used clothing are doing new service as weights for colored strips, evoking an African healer's cloak. The pockets symbolize the wear-er/donors; the whole celebrates salvage, diversity, inclusiveness, culture, and health-giving vibrations.

UNEXPECTED BABY QUILT

HOGSCREENING, VINYL, WOOL, CANE, CLOTHESPINS, ROOFING NAILS, FISHING
LINE, AND BATTING; QUILTED WITH ROOFING NAILS AND FISHING LINE; 40 X
40 INCHES.

For years I have collected various materials common to everyday life, but not typically destined for quilt making. These materials provide unique and interesting metaphors for aspects outside their ordinary context. My work seems to translate the traditional to the contemporary while pushing the boundaries of the conventional quilted form.

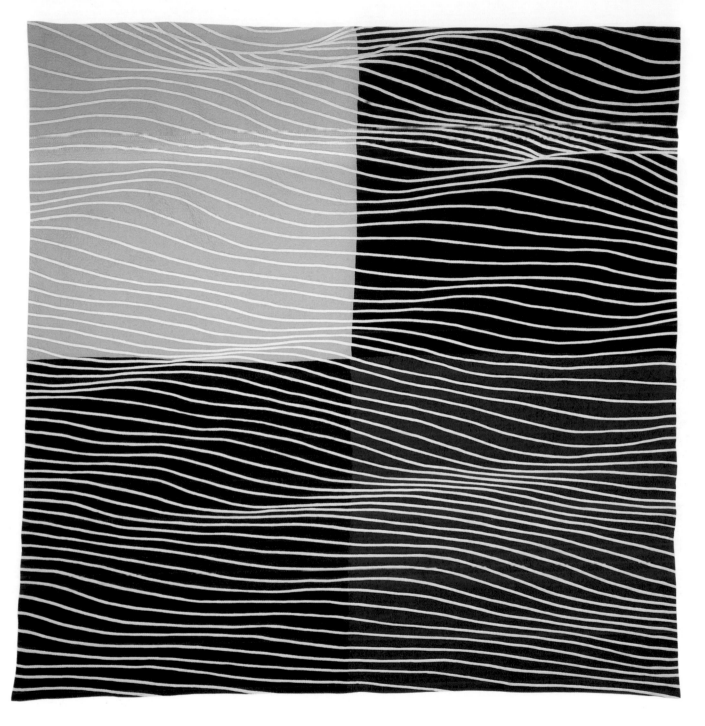

WAVES

COTTON FABRIC AND BIAS TAPE; MACHINE PIECED AND MACHINE QUILTED; 72 X 72 INCHES.

I wanted to experiment with wave-like designs and create a three-dimensional impression. The design was inspired by Robert Dixon's Mathographics.

TRAILBLAZER AWARD

I'm Buggin'

HAND-DYED (BY ARTIST AND CYNTHIA BONNER) COTTON FABRIC; MACHINE
APPLIQUÉD AND MACHINE QUILTED; 51 X 50 INCHES.

For the past year, I have been working on whimsical quilts that depict images of important objects in my life. The Volkswagen bug was an especially fun quilt to make, bringing back memories of the cream-colored bug I had in college that my friends affectionately nicknamed "The Egg."

ABOUT THE DAIRY BARN

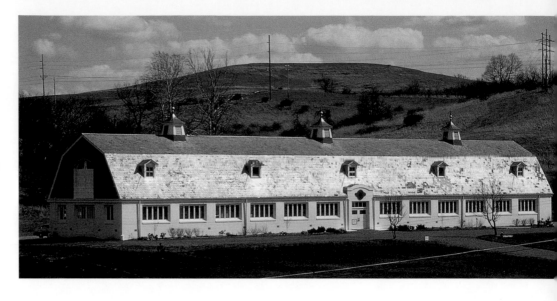

The Dairy Barn Southeastern Ohio Cultural Arts Center, a unique arts facility in the Appalachian foothills, has showcased regional, national, and international arts and crafts since 1978. Its year-round calendar of events includes international juried exhibits, programs and exhibits of regional interest, festivals, performances, special activities and arts education classes for children and adults.

The history of the Dairy Barn is as colorful as its exhibits. Built in 1914, the structure housed an active dairy herd until the late 1960s. Ten years later, local artists and art lovers Harriet and Ora Anderson recognized the building's potential as a much-needed regional arts center, and they worked tirelessly to rally community support to save the idle, dilapidated structure. With only nine days to spare, the demolition order was reversed. The building was placed on the National Register of Historic Places, and the Dairy Barn Southeastern Ohio Cultural Arts Center was born.

Through several renovation projects, the architects retained the original character of the building as it evolved from a seasonal, makeshift exhibit space into a first-class, fully-accessible arts facility with a 7,000-square-foot gallery that also includes the specially equipped Ann Howland Arts Education Center. In 1995, the Dairy Barn received a State of Ohio grant that will enable the start of the ultimate transformation of the upper level for additional classrooms, a meeting area, a performance space, an exhibit preparation space, and an always-needed storage area.

Quilt National '95 installations.

The Dairy Barn is supported by admissions, memberships, corporate sponsorships, grants, and donations. The staff is assisted by a large group of volunteers who annually donate thousands of hours of time and talent. For a calendar of events and information about other Dairy Barn programs, contact the Dairy Barn Arts Center, P.O. Box 747, Athens, Ohio, 45701 USA; phone 614/592-4981; or visit the World Wide Web site at http://www.eurekanet.com/~dbarn.

SHOW ITINERARY

The complete **Quilt National '97** collection will be on display from May 24 through September 1, 1997 at the Dairy Barn Southeastern Ohio Cultural Arts Center, 8000 Dairy Lane, Athens, Ohio. Three separate groups of **Quilt National '97** works will then begin a two-year tour of museums and galleries. Host venues will display only a portion of the full **Quilt National '97** collection.

Tentative dates (unless otherwise noted) and locations are listed below. For an updated itinerary or to receive additional information about hosting a **Quilt National** touring collection, contact the Dairy Barn Cultural Arts Center, P. O. Box 747, Athens, Ohio, 45701-0747. Phone: 614-592-4981. FAX: 614-592-5090. World Wide Web site: http://www.eurekanet.com/~dbarn.

❖10/1 - 11/1/97
St Louis, MO; Benefit for the Women's Self Help Center, site to be announced (B & C)

❖10/23 - 10/26/97
Houston, TX; George Brown Convention Center, Int'l Quilt Festival (A)

❖2/6 - 4/3/98
Lewisburg, WV; Carnegie Hall (A)

2/25 - 4/5/98
West Bend, WI; West Bend Art Museum (B) ❖❖

❖5/1 - 6/15/98
Bloomingdale, IL; Bloomingdale Park District Museum (A) ❖❖

5/7 - 6/28/98
San Jose, CA; American Museum of Quilts & Textiles (C) ❖❖

5/25 - 5/31/98
Insbruck, Austria; Quilt Expo VI (B) ❖❖

6/25 - 9/3/98
Ashland, OR; Schneider Museum of Art (B) ❖❖

❖7/1 - 7/31/98
Waverly, IA; Wartburg College, Waldemar A. Schmidt Gallery (A) ❖❖

11/7/98 - 1/3/99
Wausau, WI; Leigh Yawkey Woodson Art Museum (C)

❖11/13/98 - 1/2/99
Lowell, MA; New England Quilt Museum (B)

❖1/22 - 4/4/99
Columbus, OH; Riffe Gallery (C) ❖❖

❖6/12 - 8/7/99
Lawrence, KS; Spencer Museum of Art (B) ❖❖

7/5 - 8/1/99
Waterville, ME; Colby College Museum (C); Cosponsored by Pine Tree Quilters

❖9/11 - 10/23/99
Bloomingdale, IL; Bloomingdale Park District Museum (B) ❖❖

Contact the Dairy Barn Cultural Arts Center for additional scheduled bookings. It is recommended that you verify this information by calling a specific host venue prior to visiting the site.

❖ site has hosted an earlier Dairy Barn touring collection
❖ ❖ denotes tentative booking

Artists' Index